I0482559

Thank you for purchasing this book. I hope it inspires you to continue creating.

The world is but a canvas to our imagination

- Henry David Thoreau

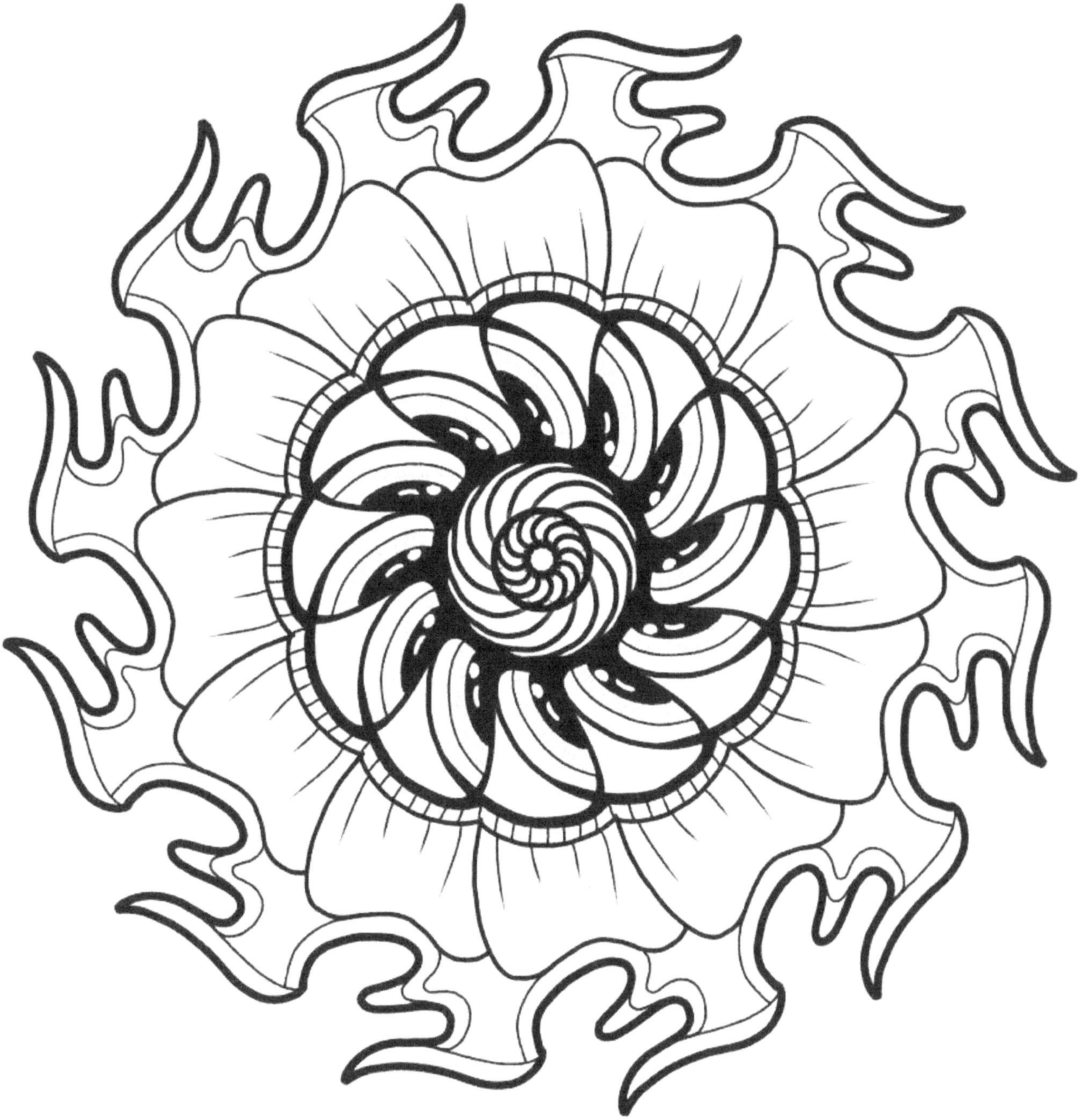

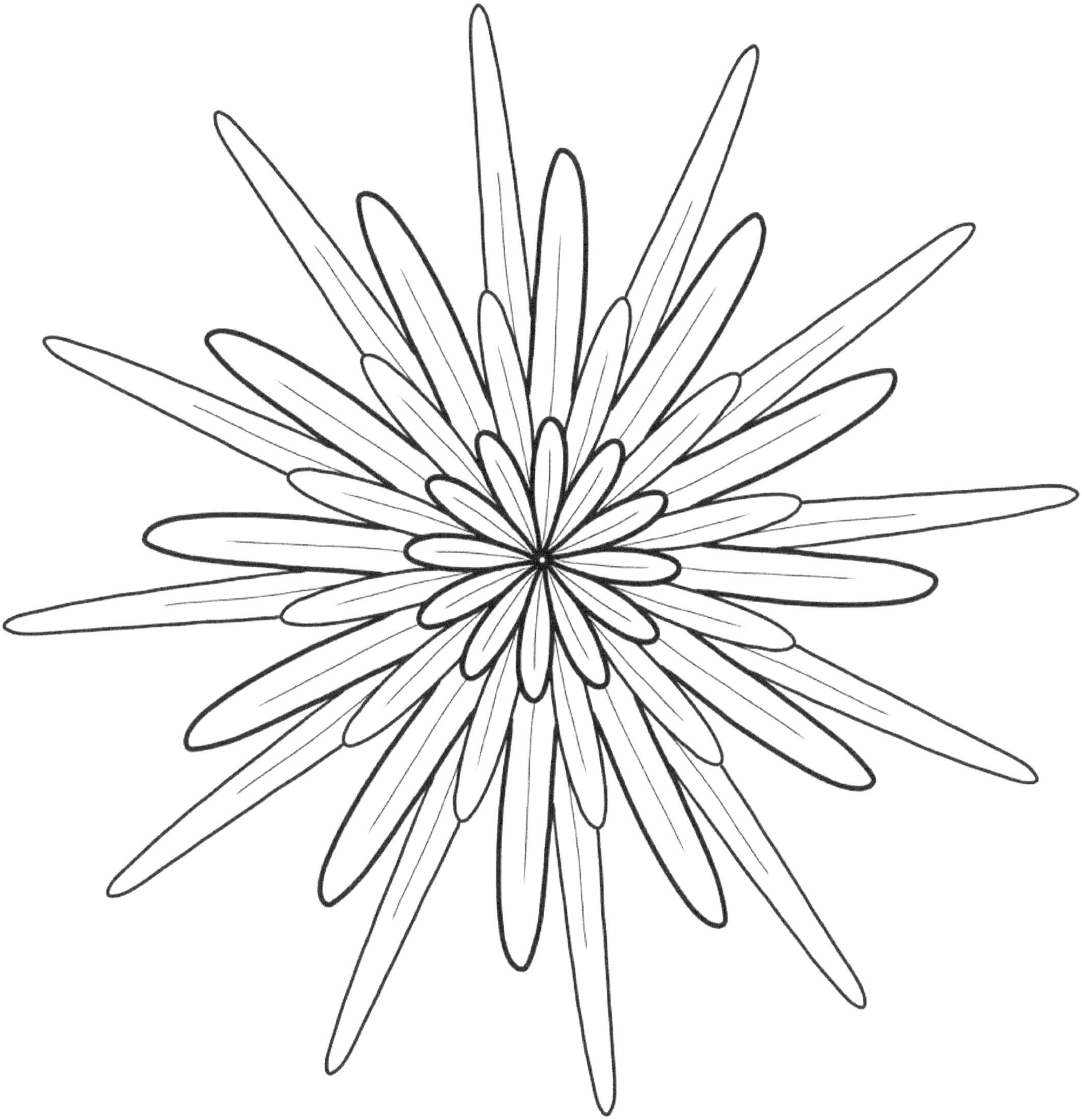

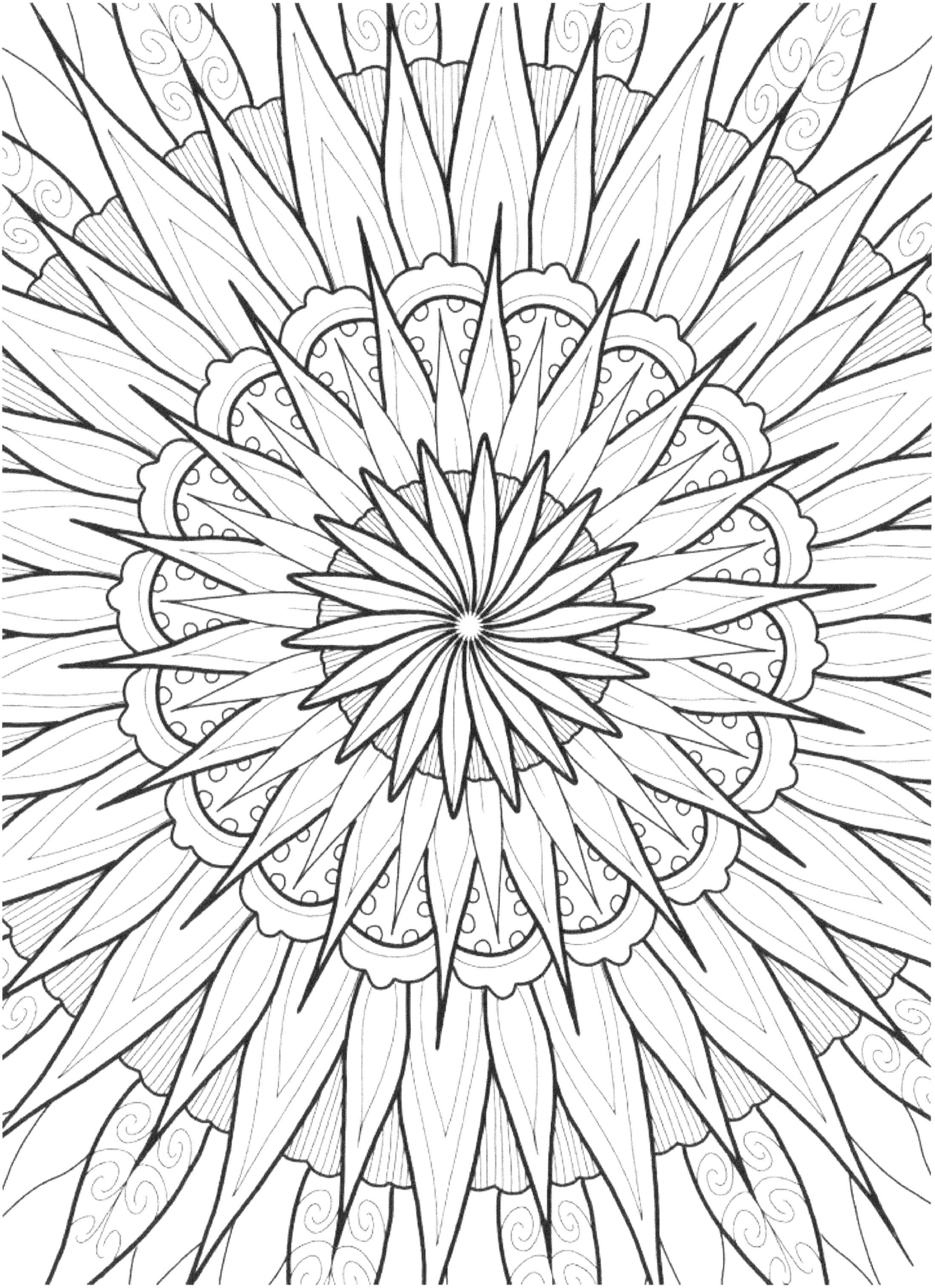

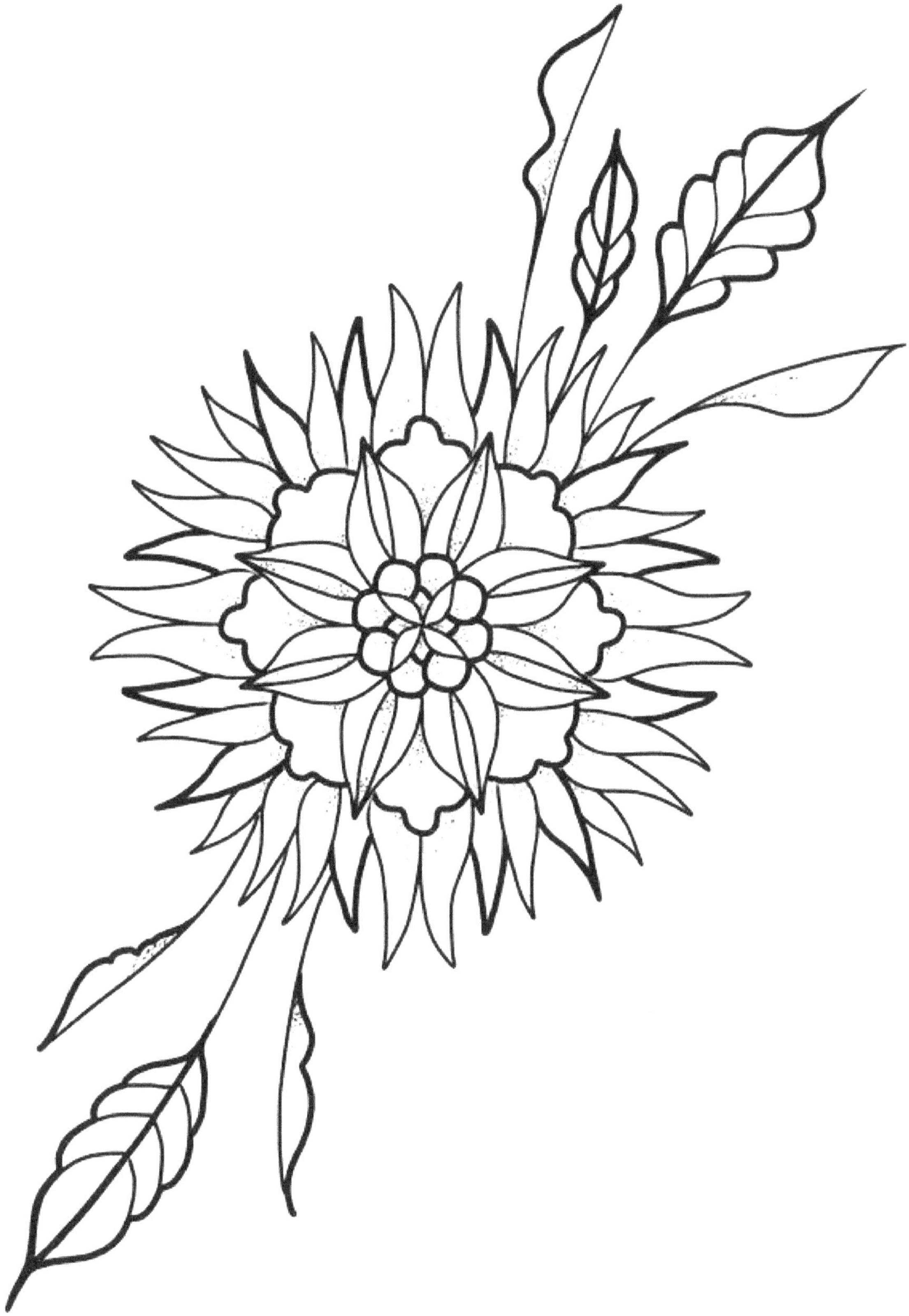

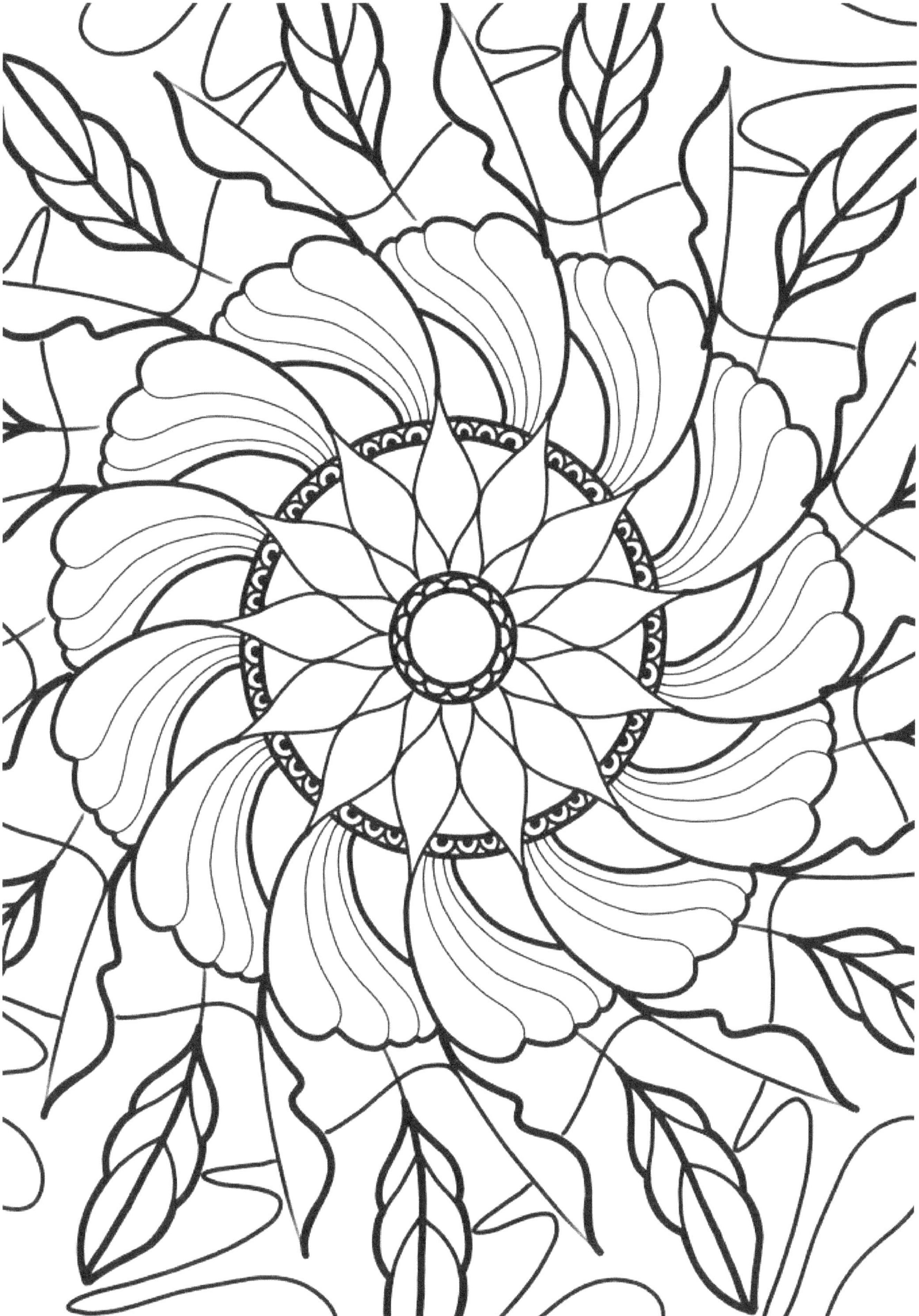

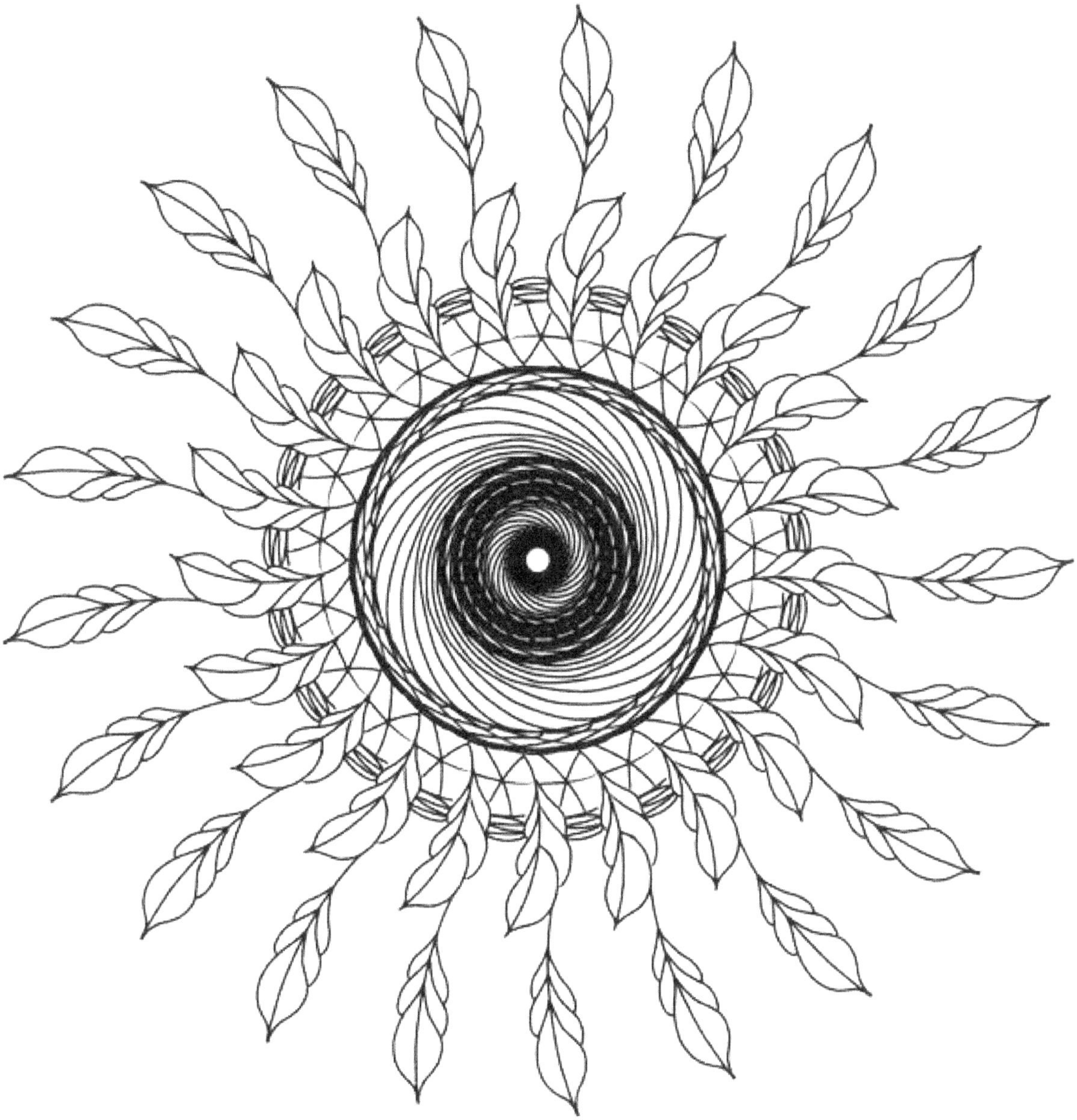

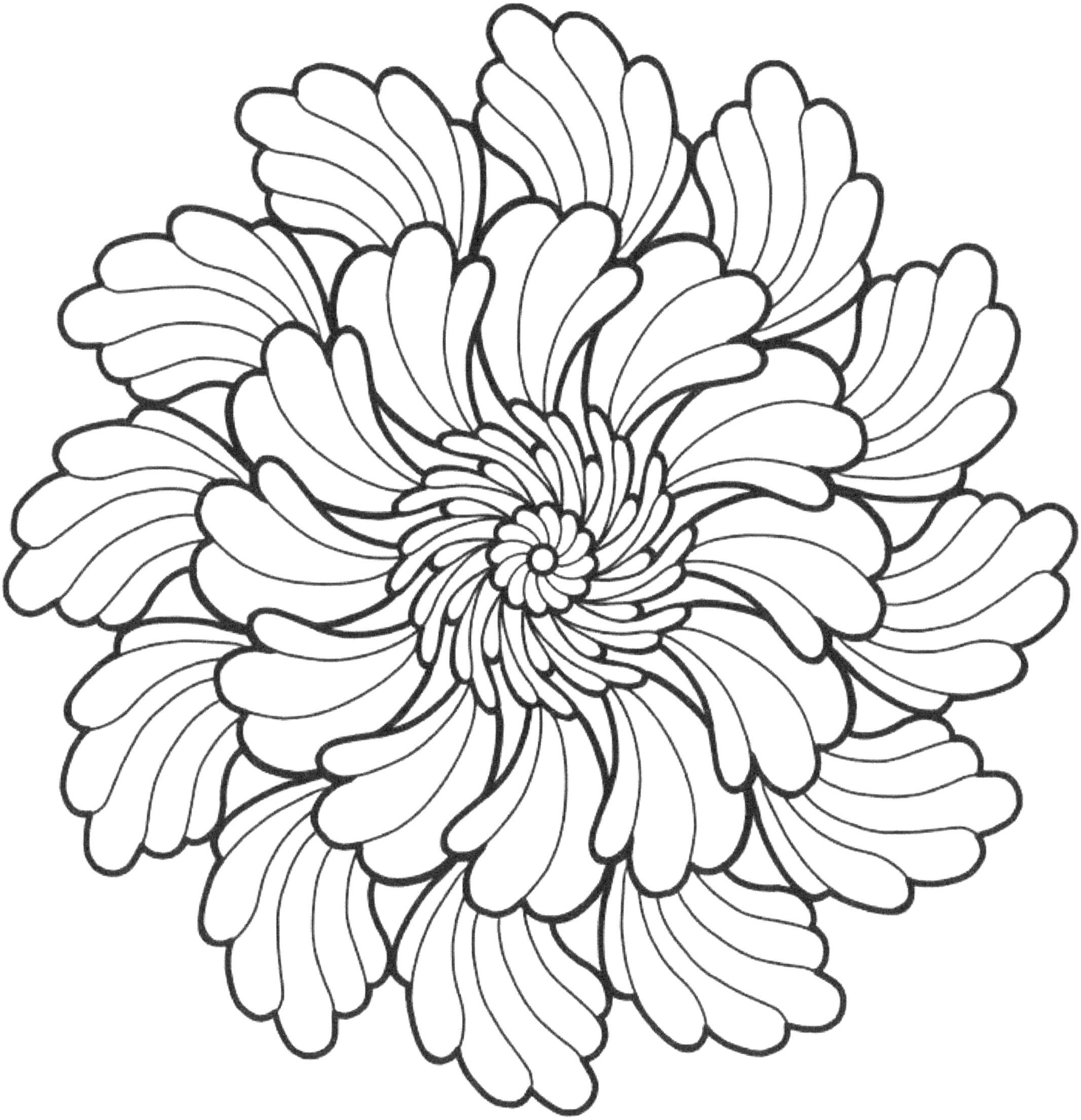

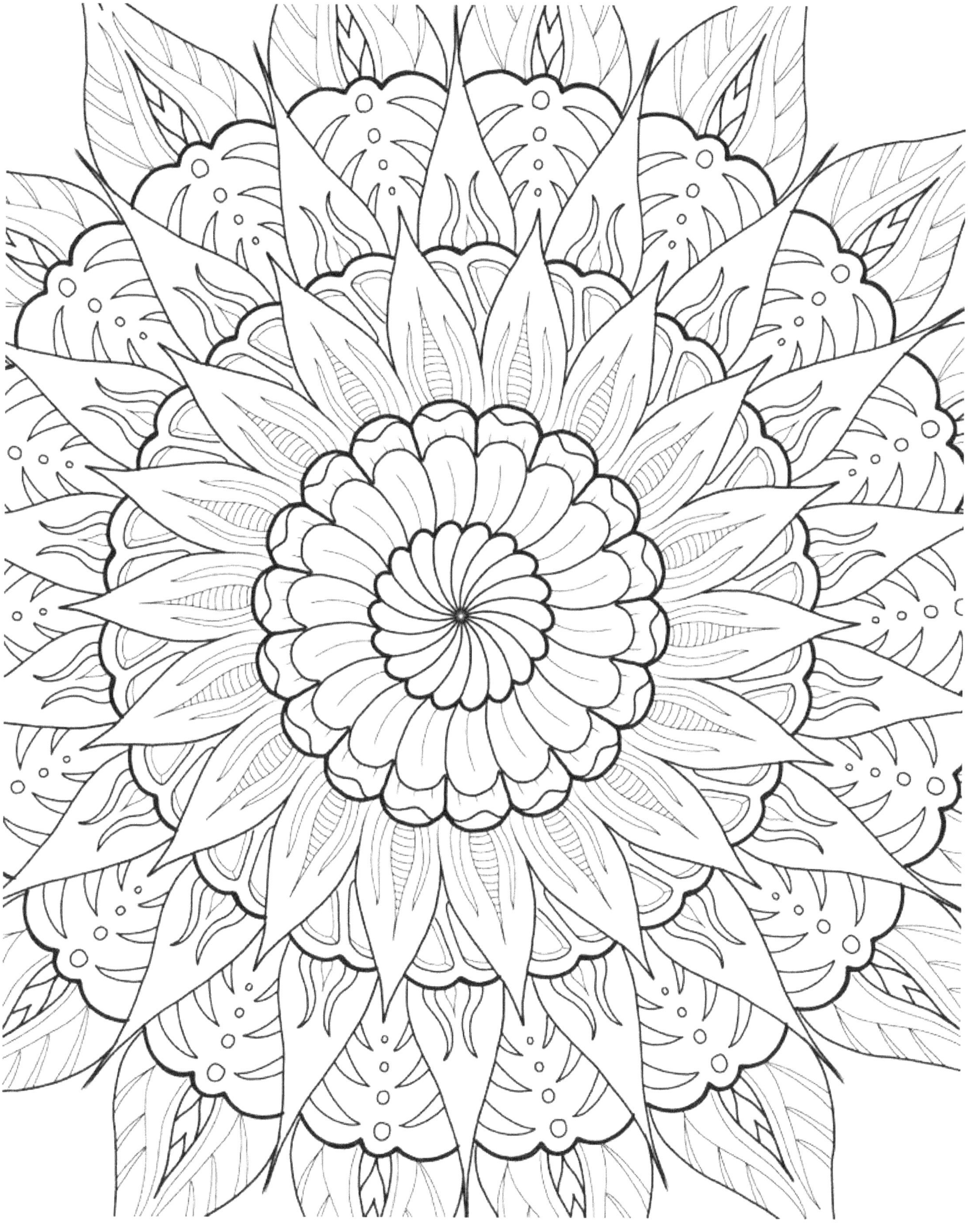

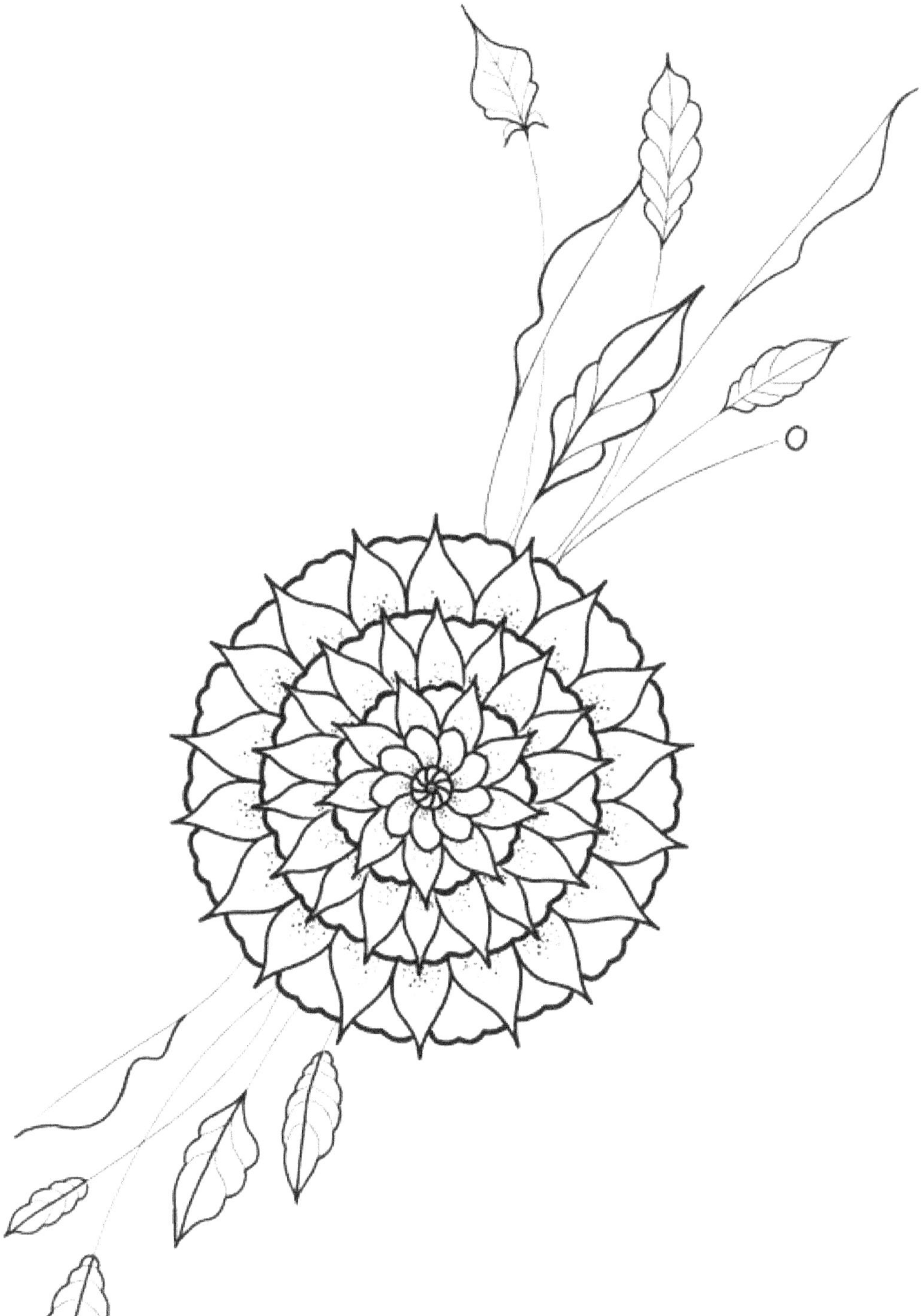

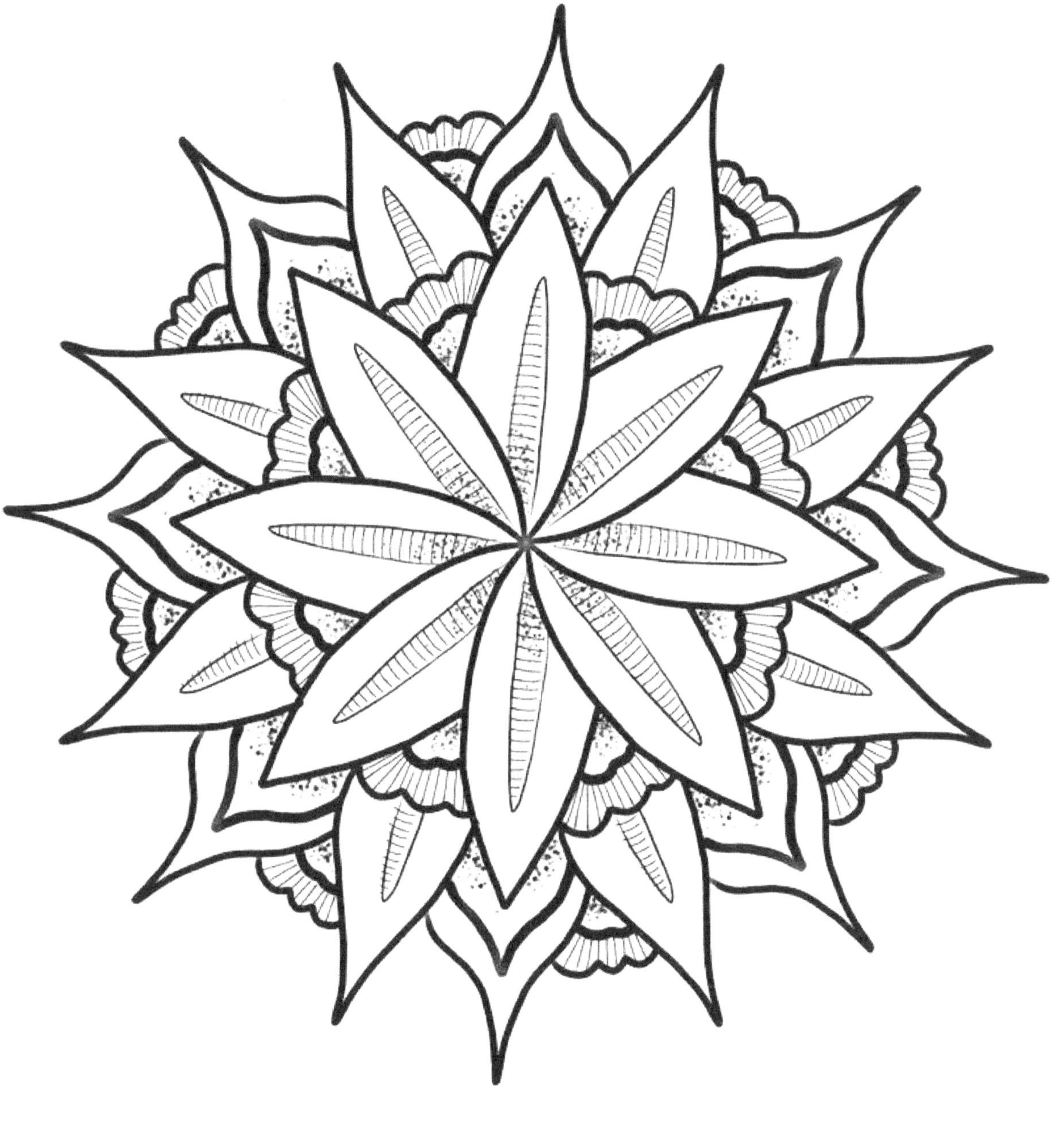

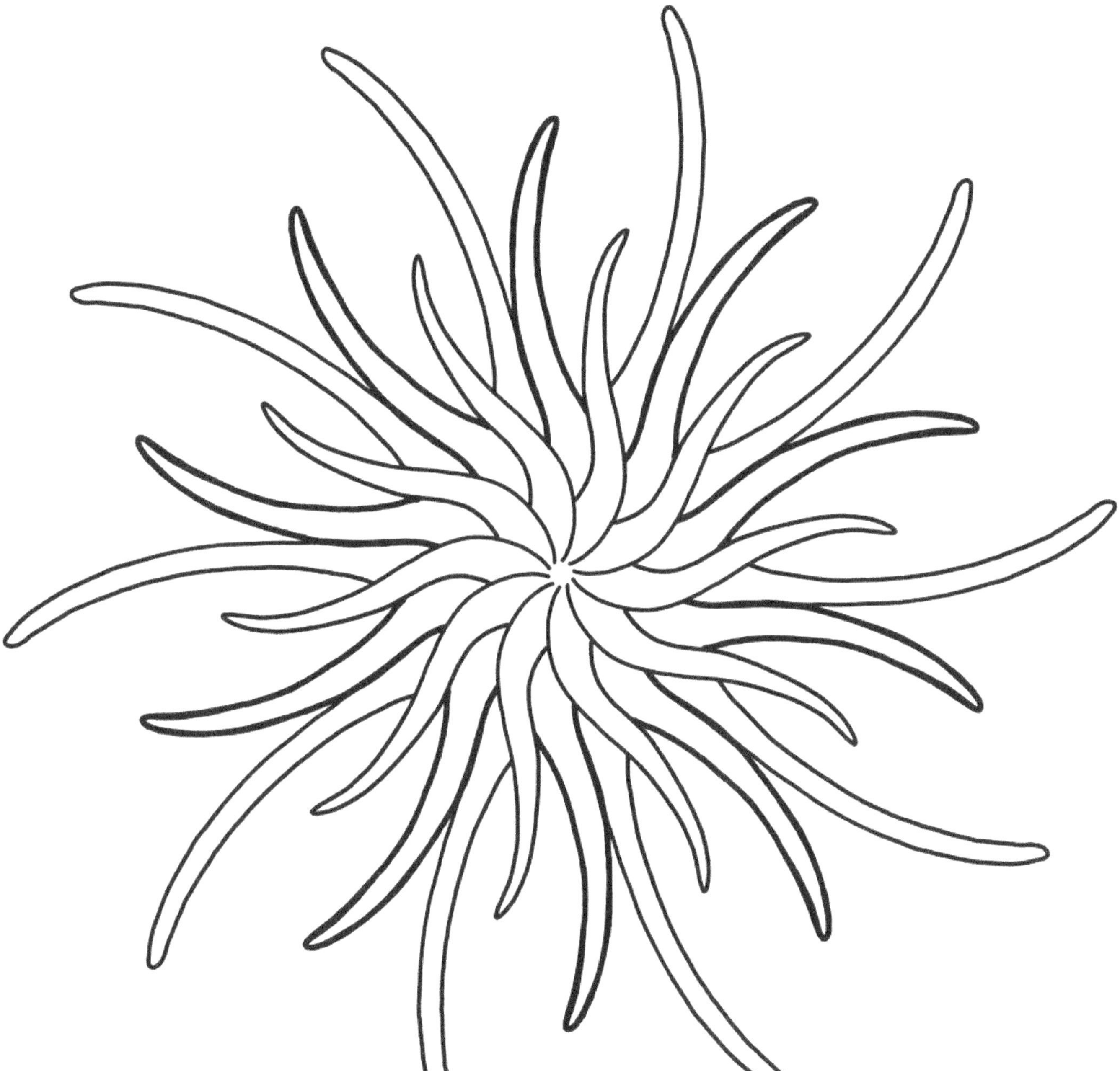

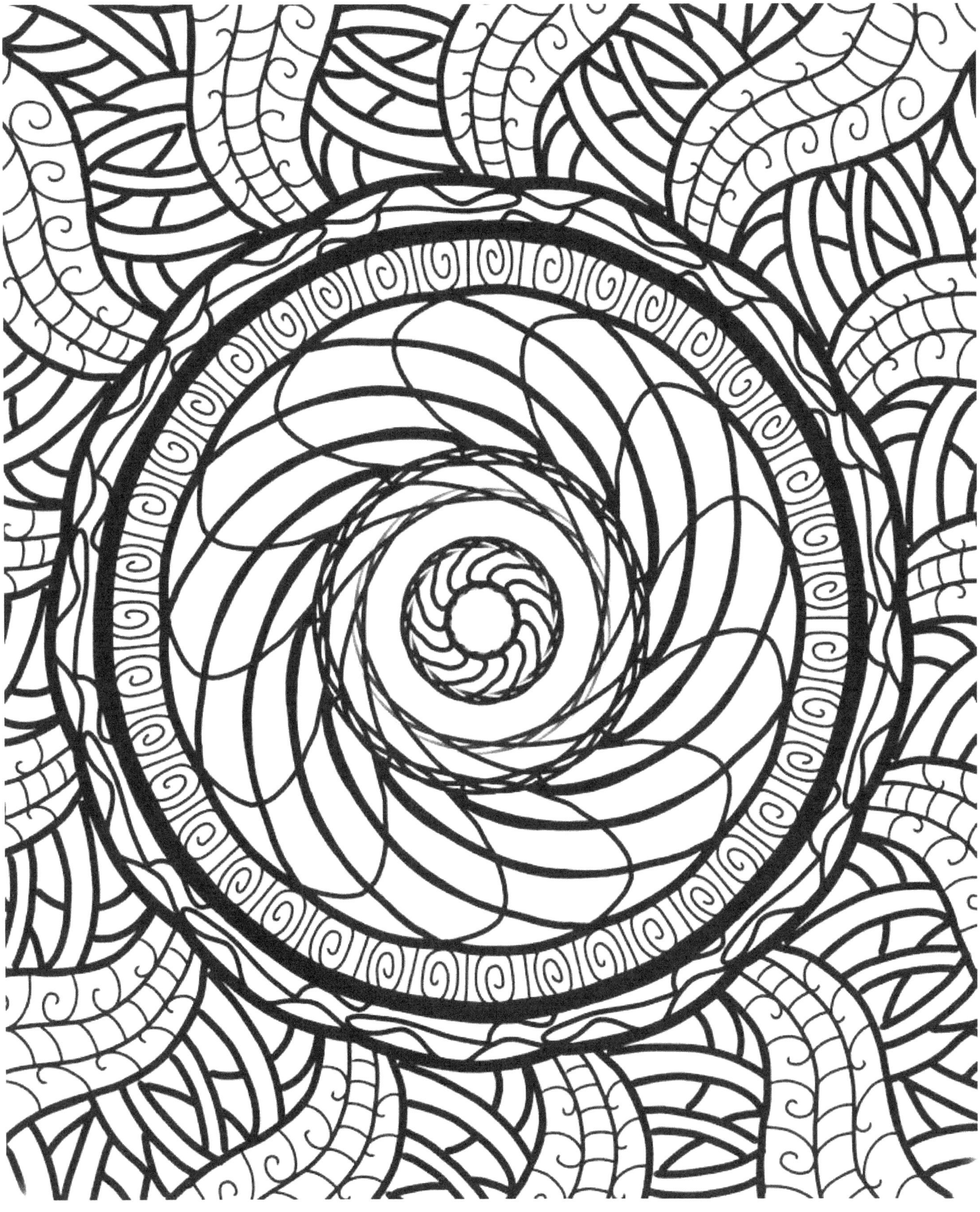

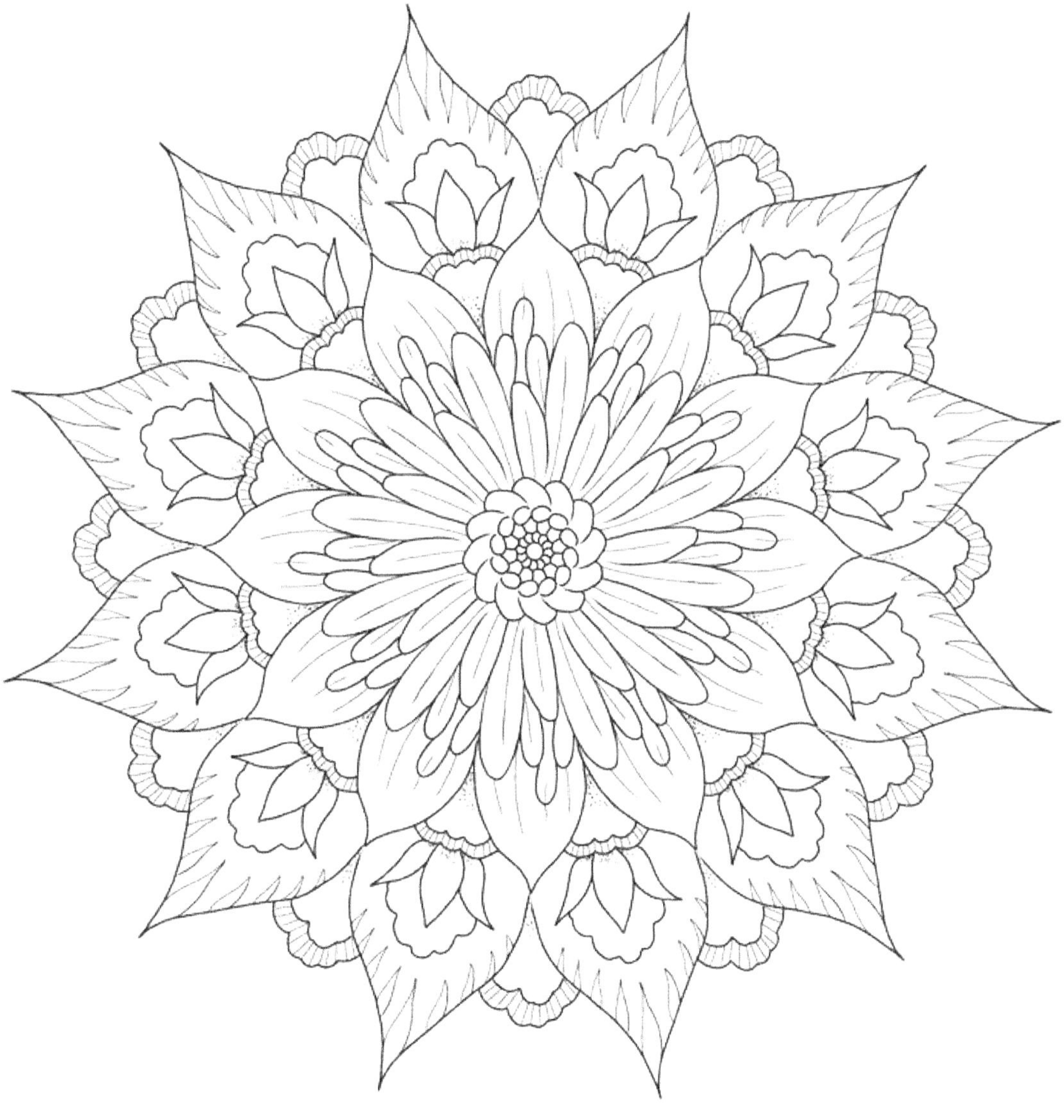

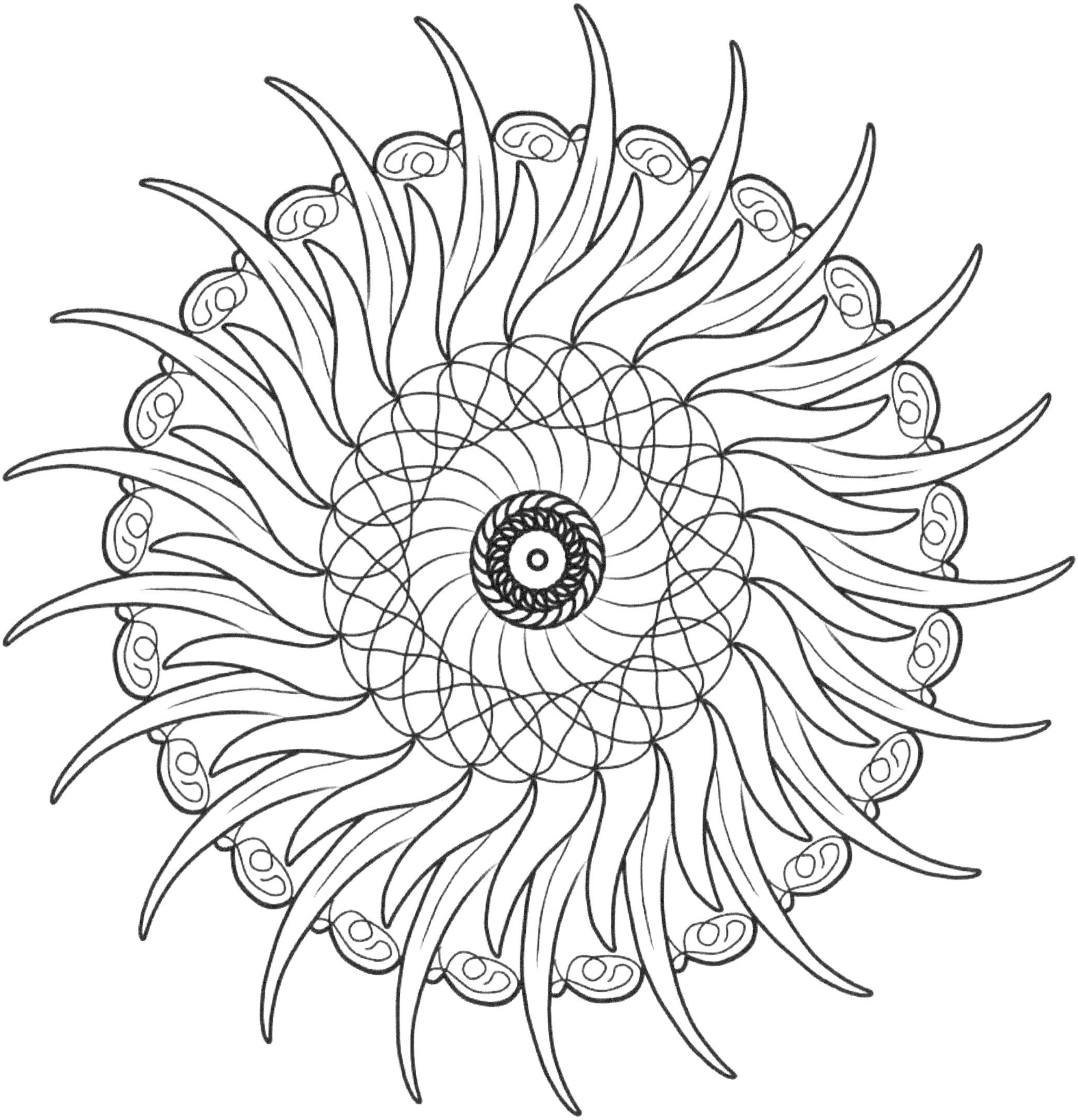

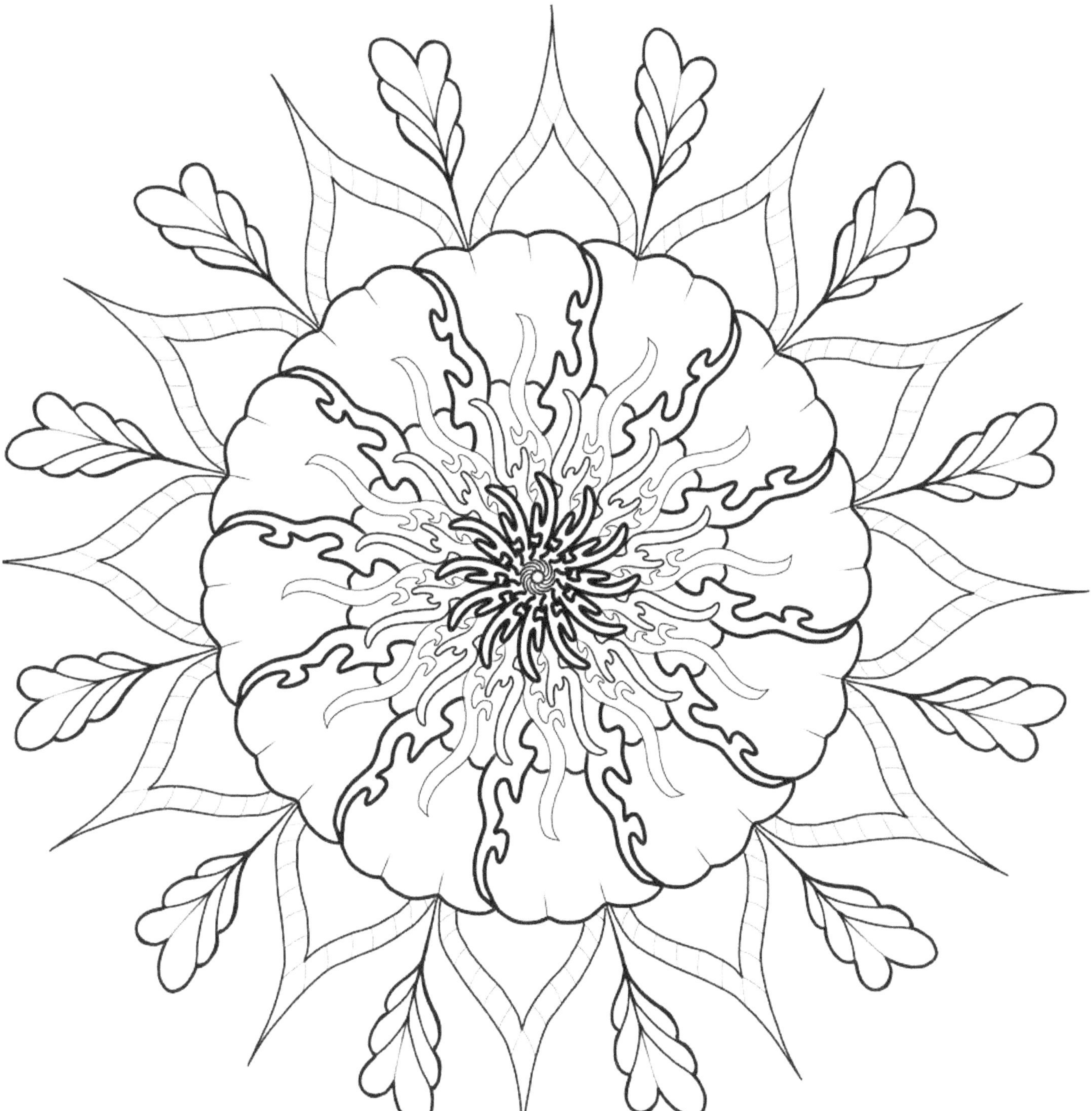

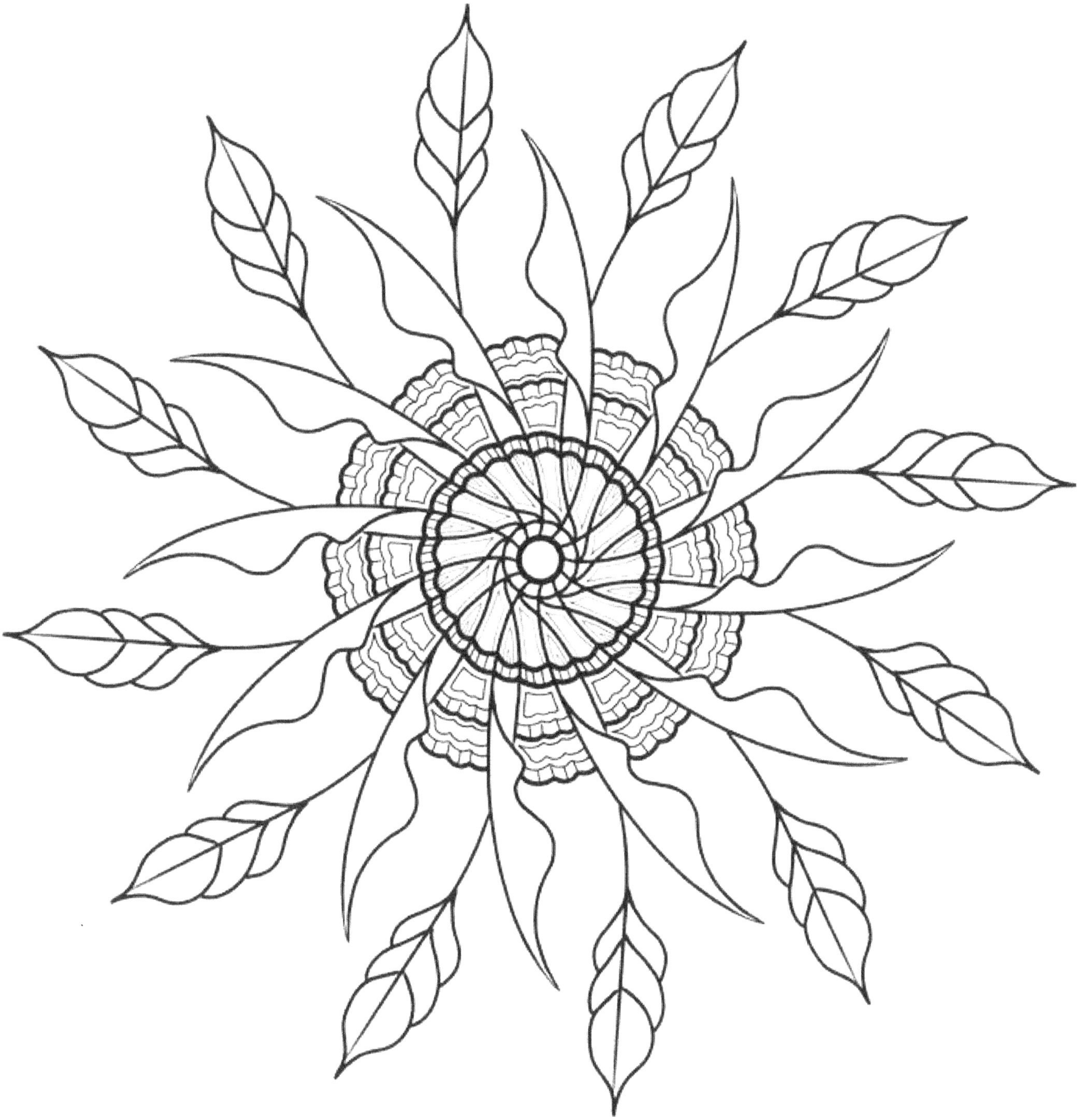

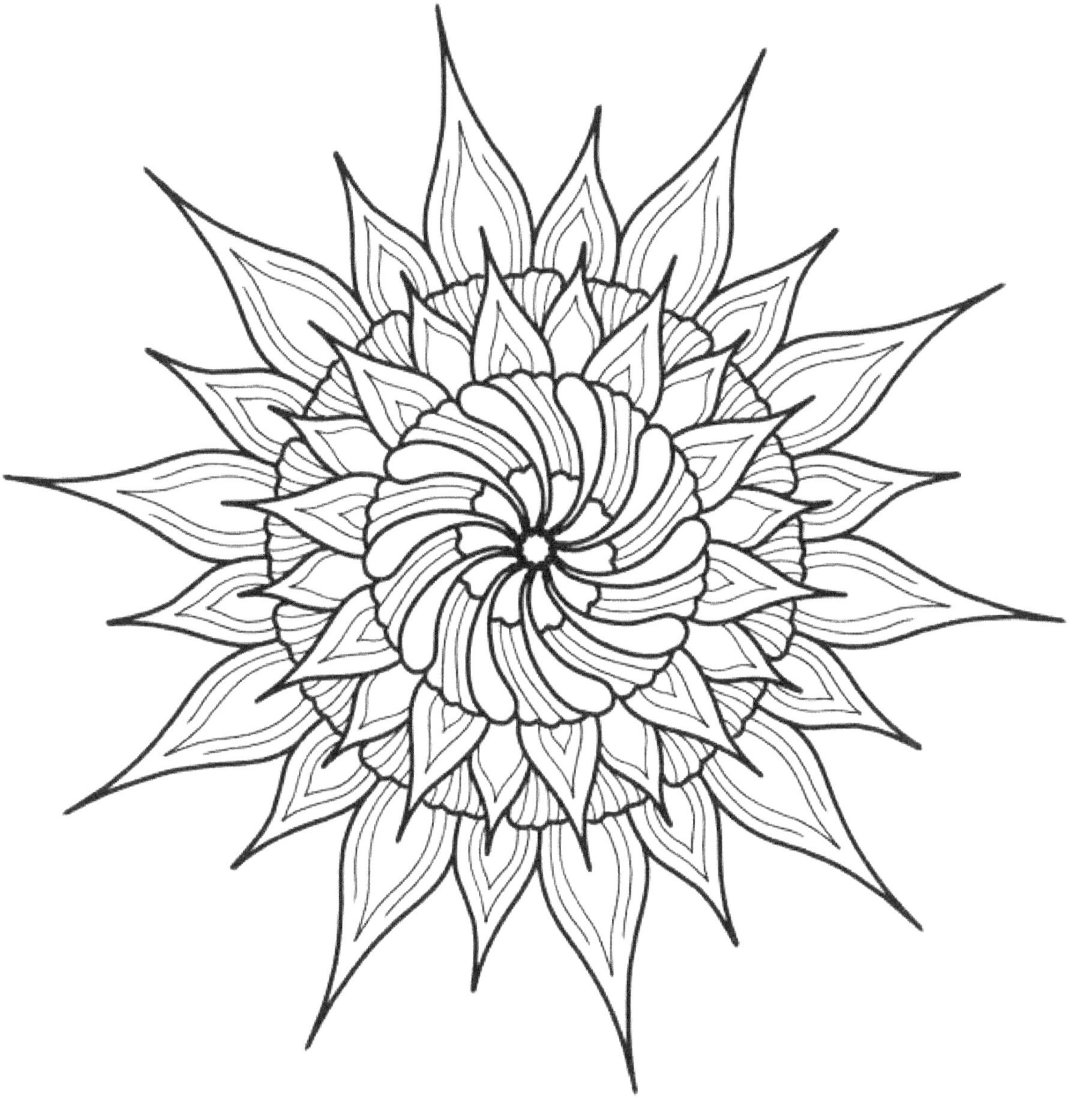

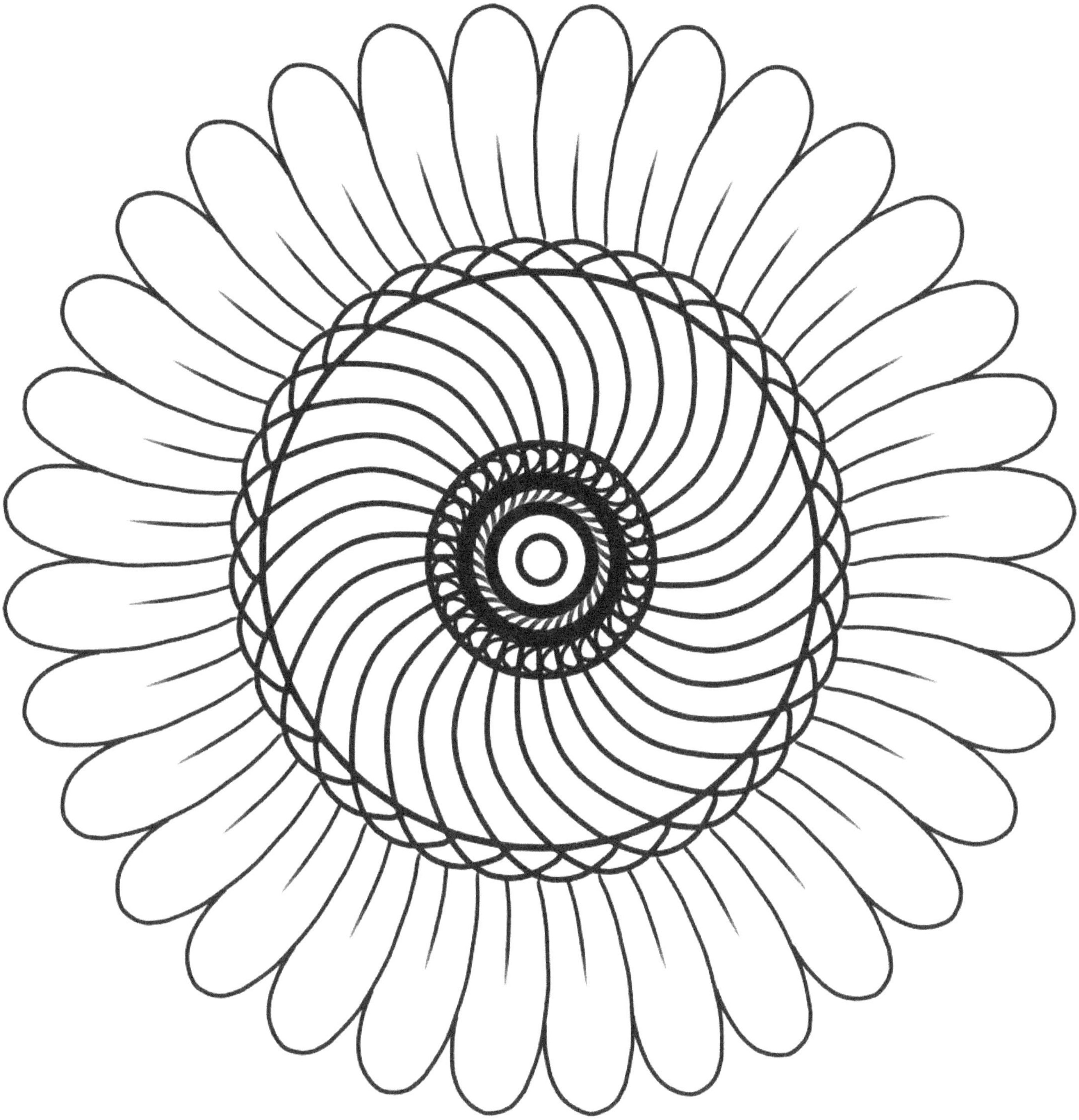

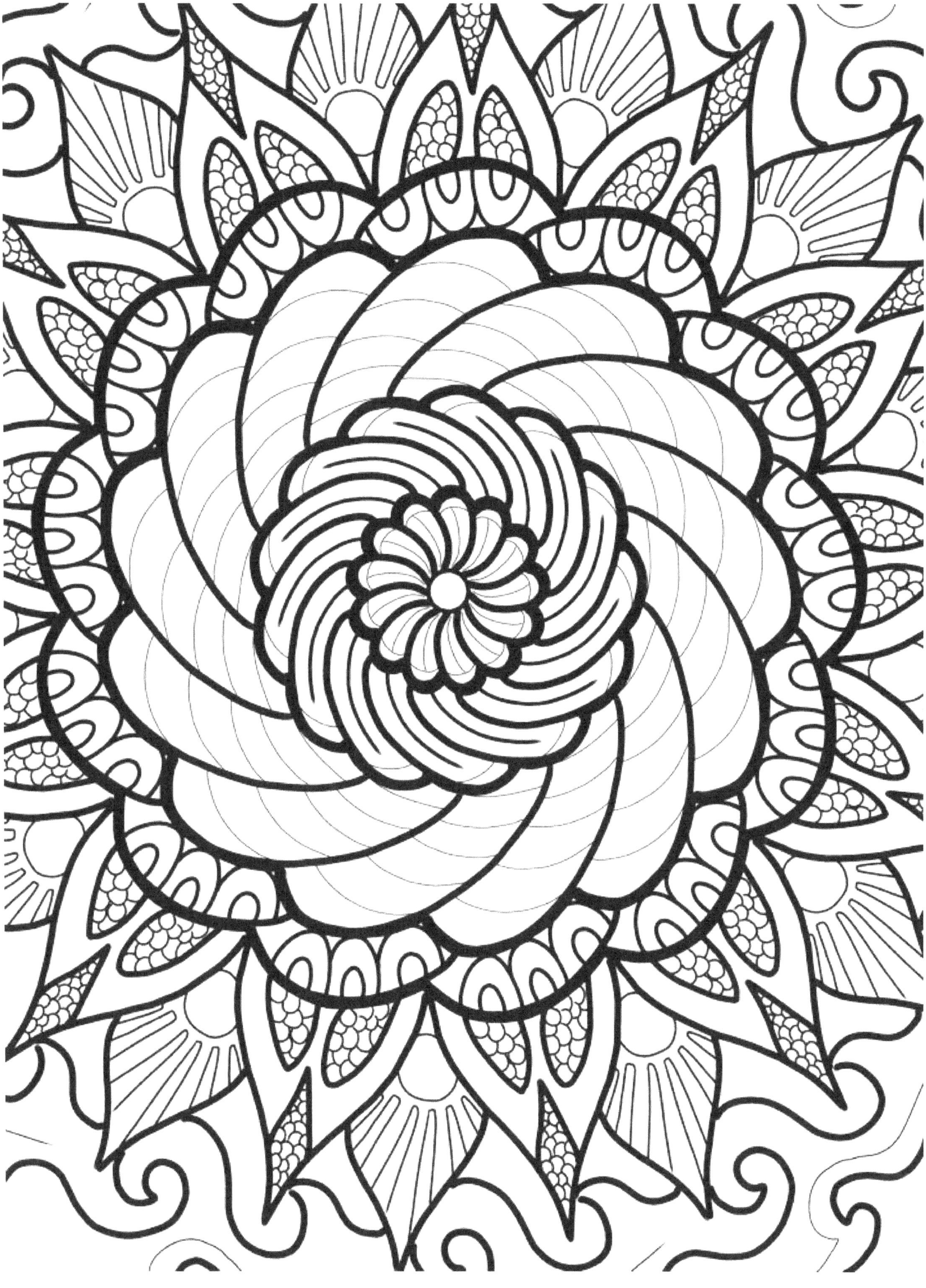

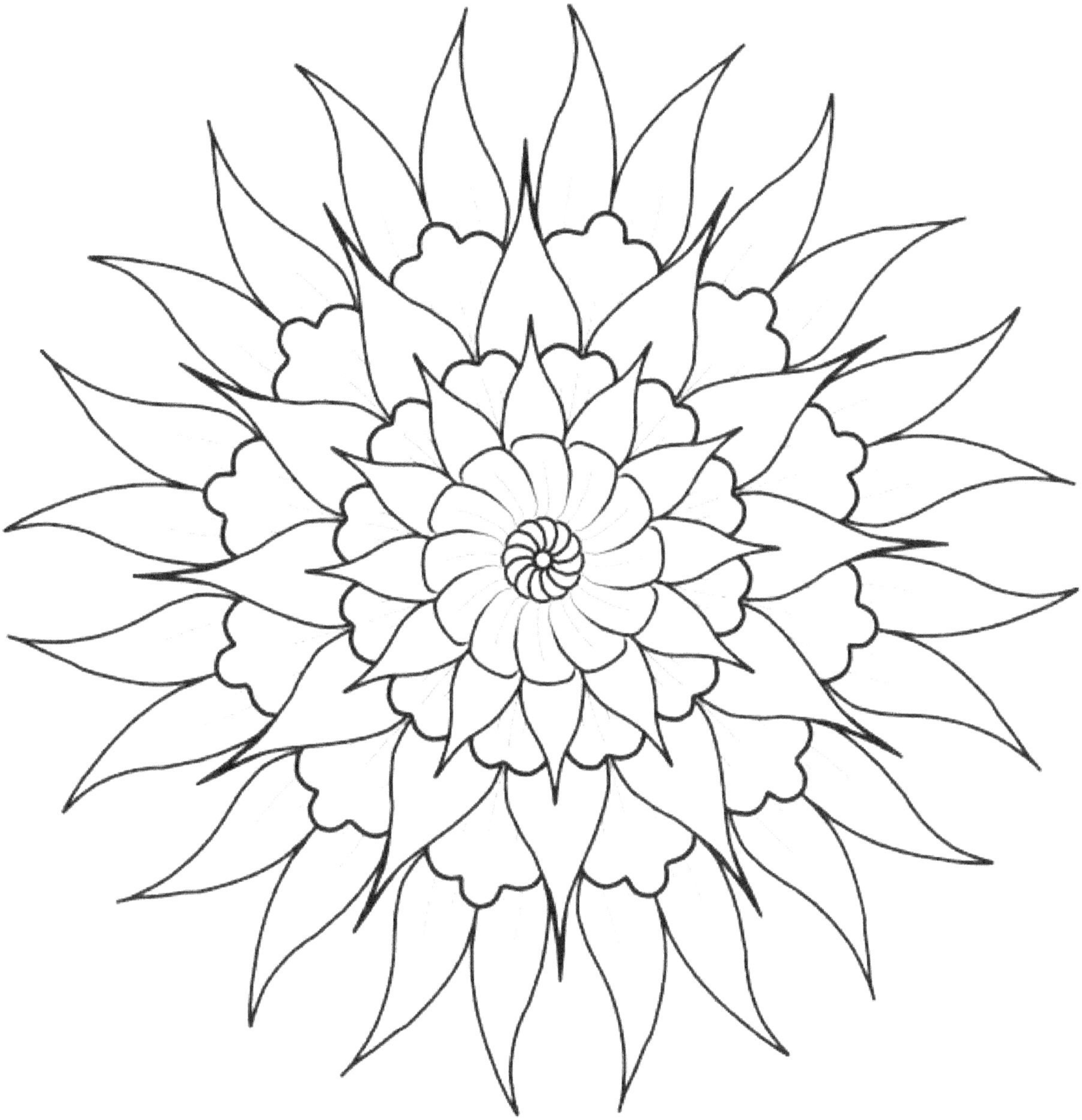

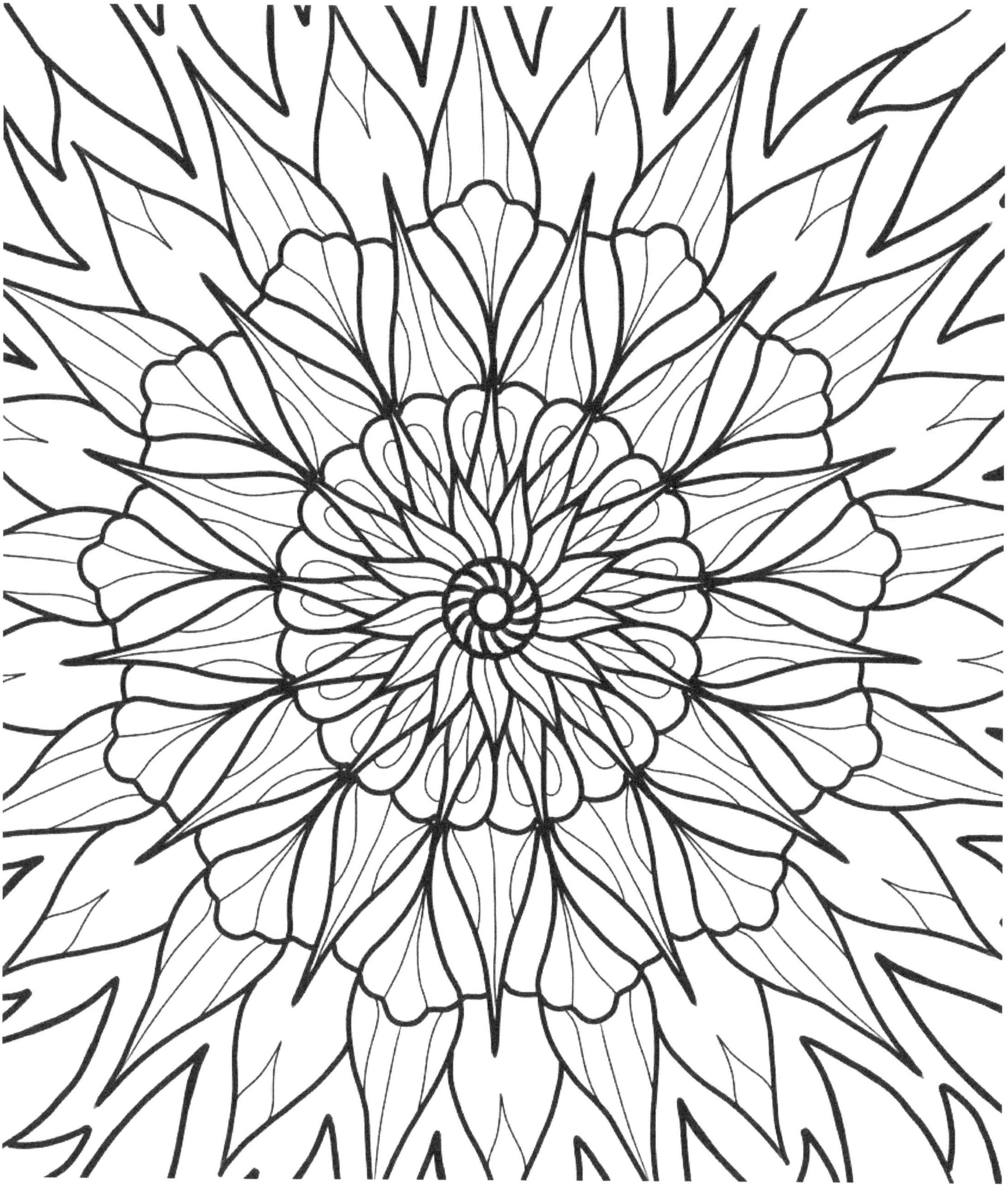

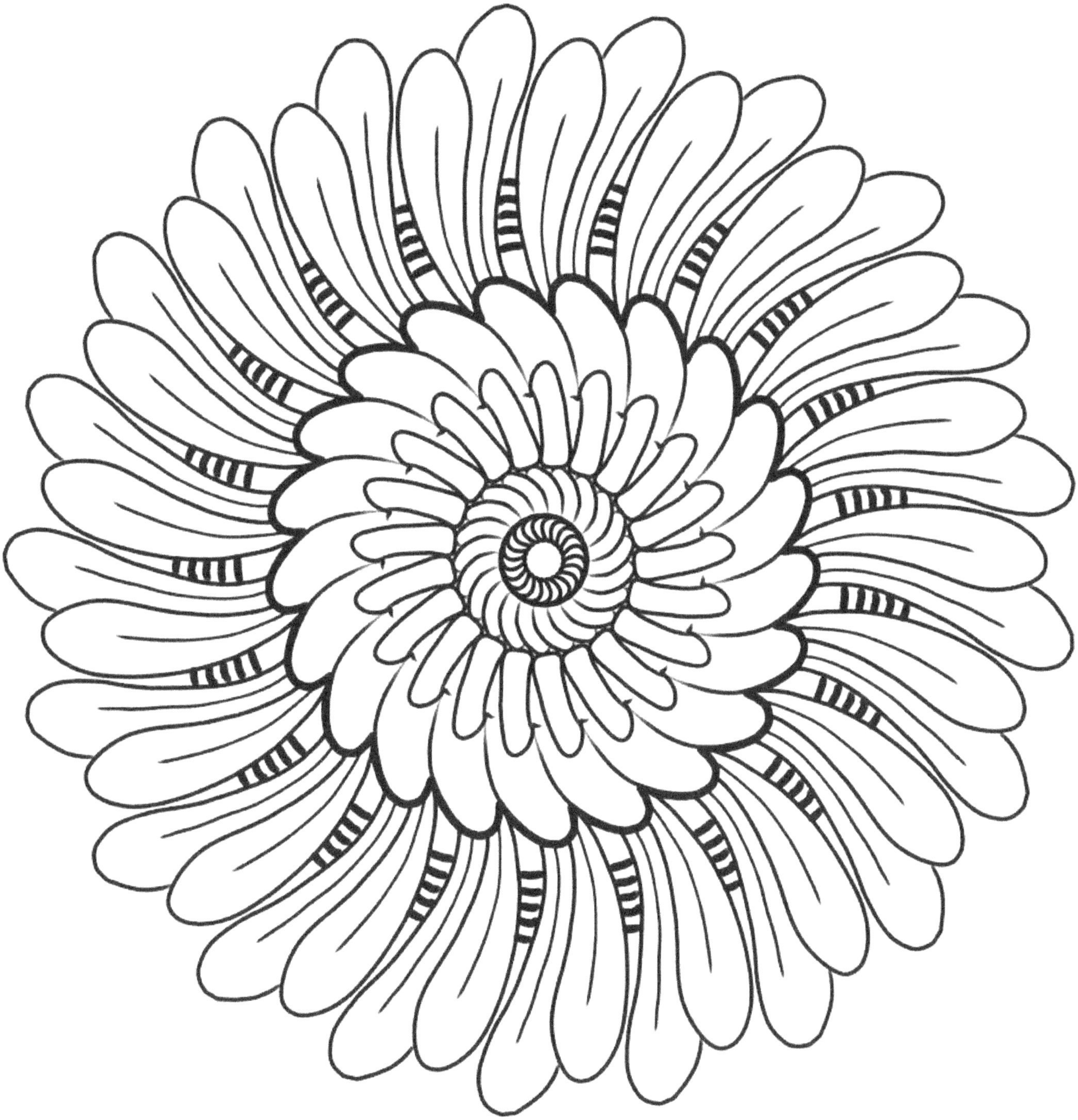

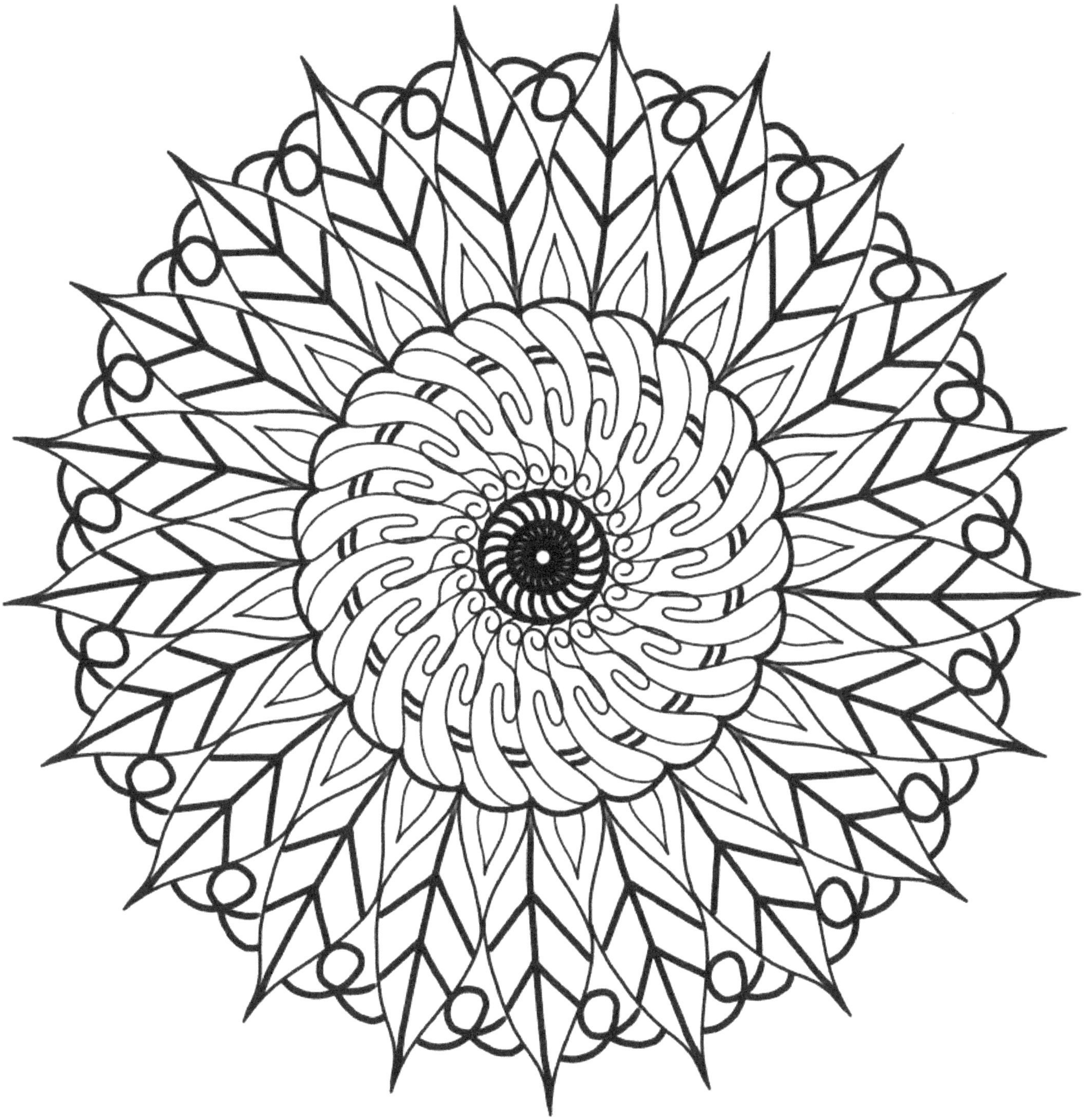

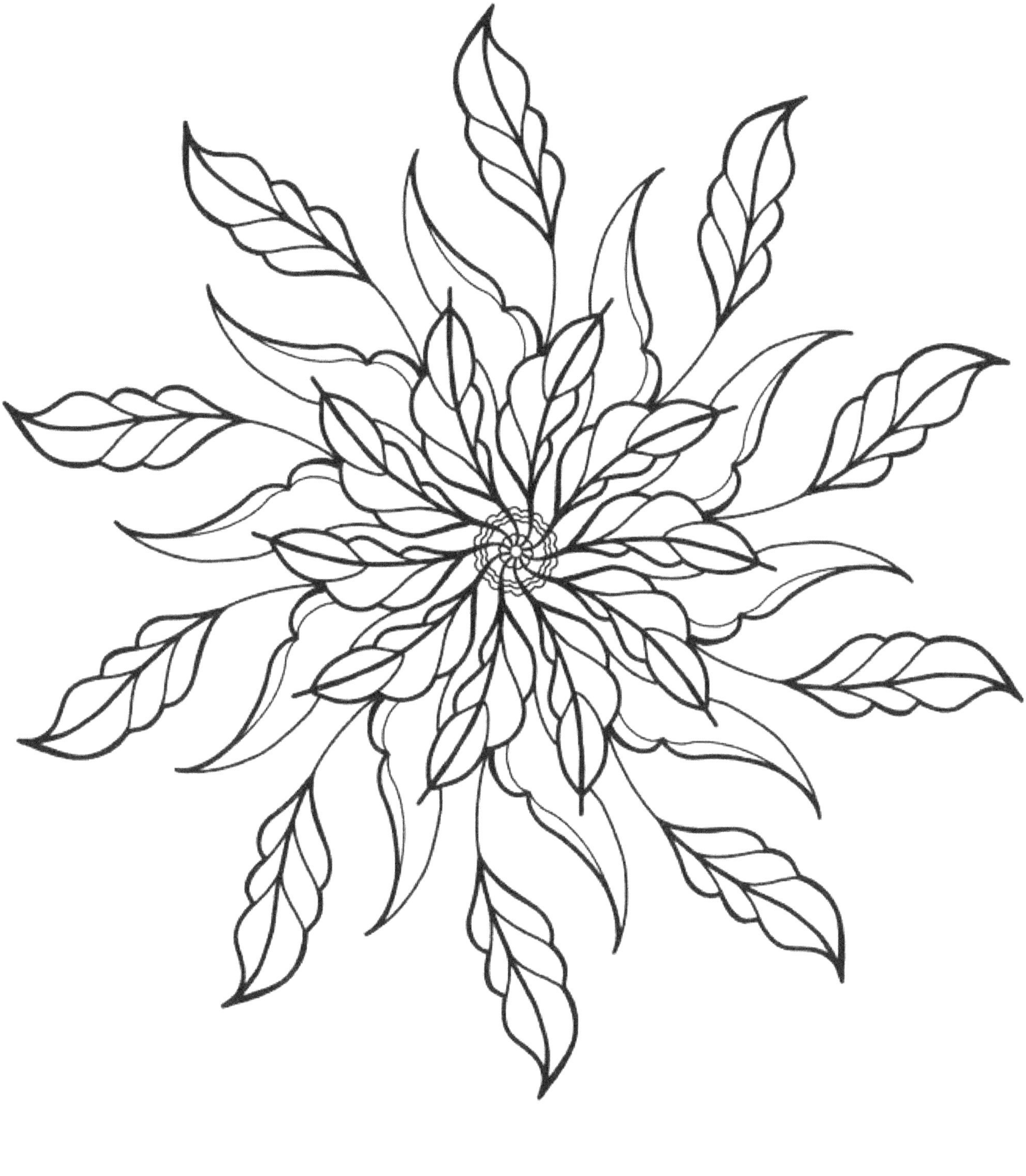

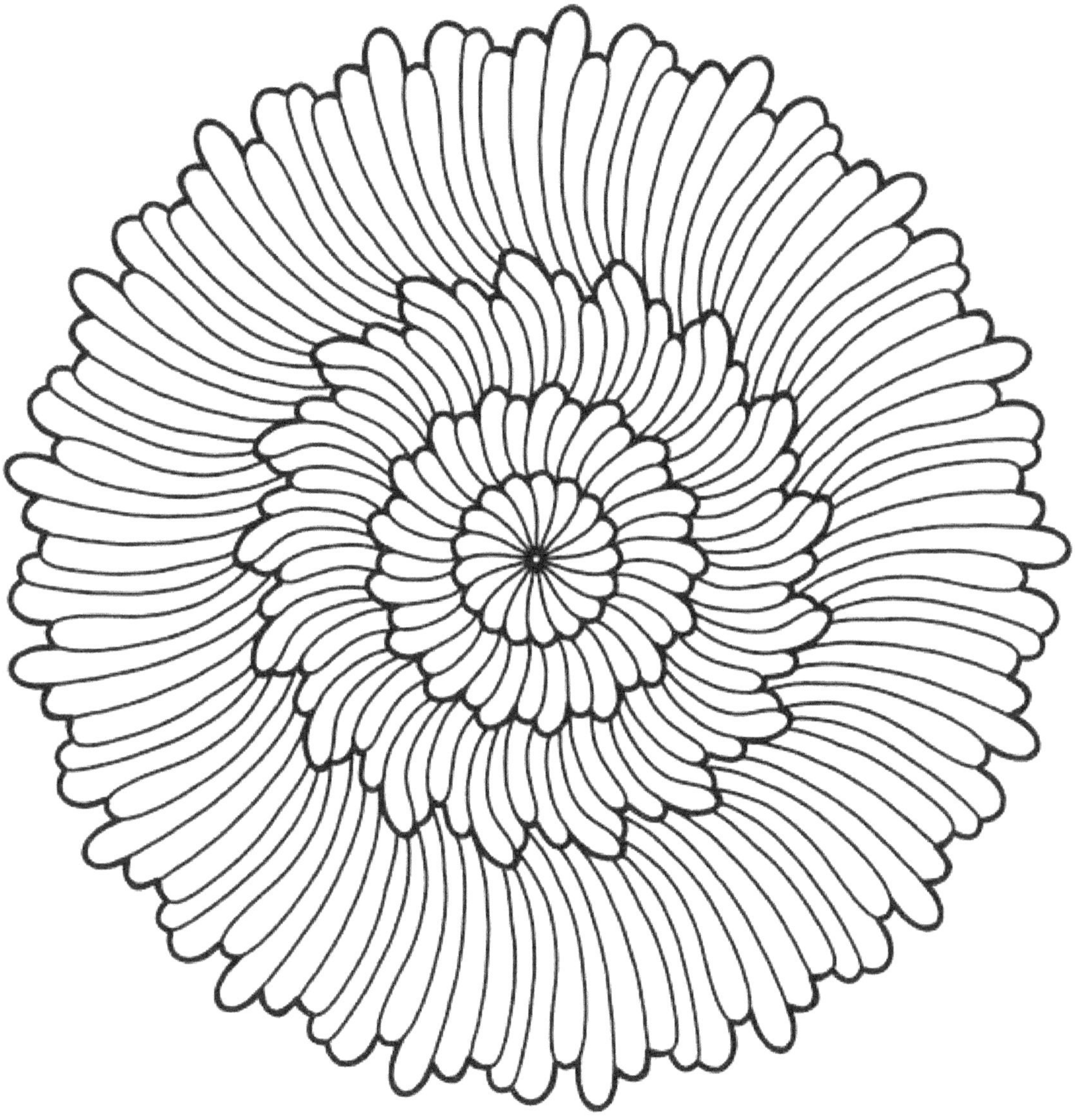

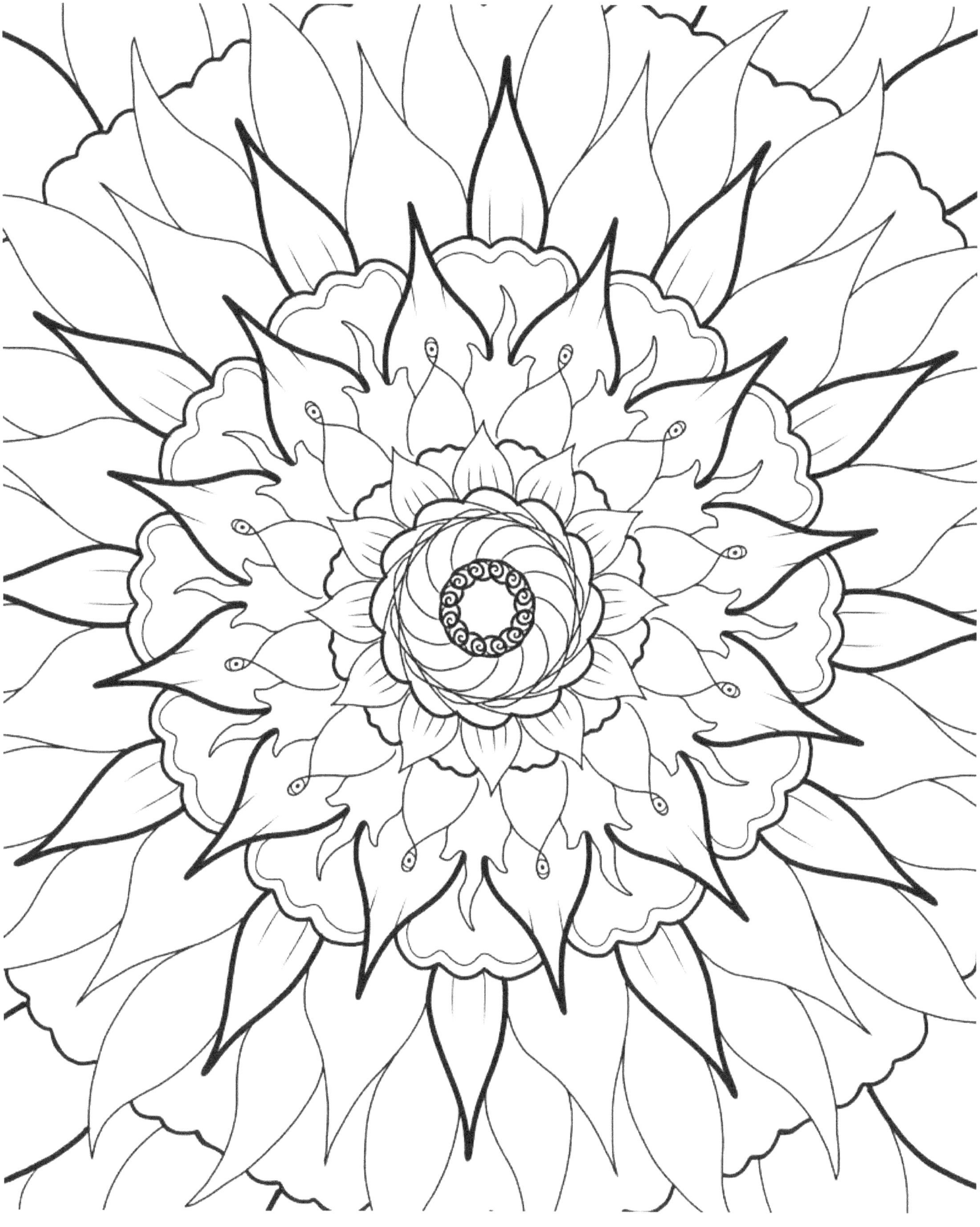

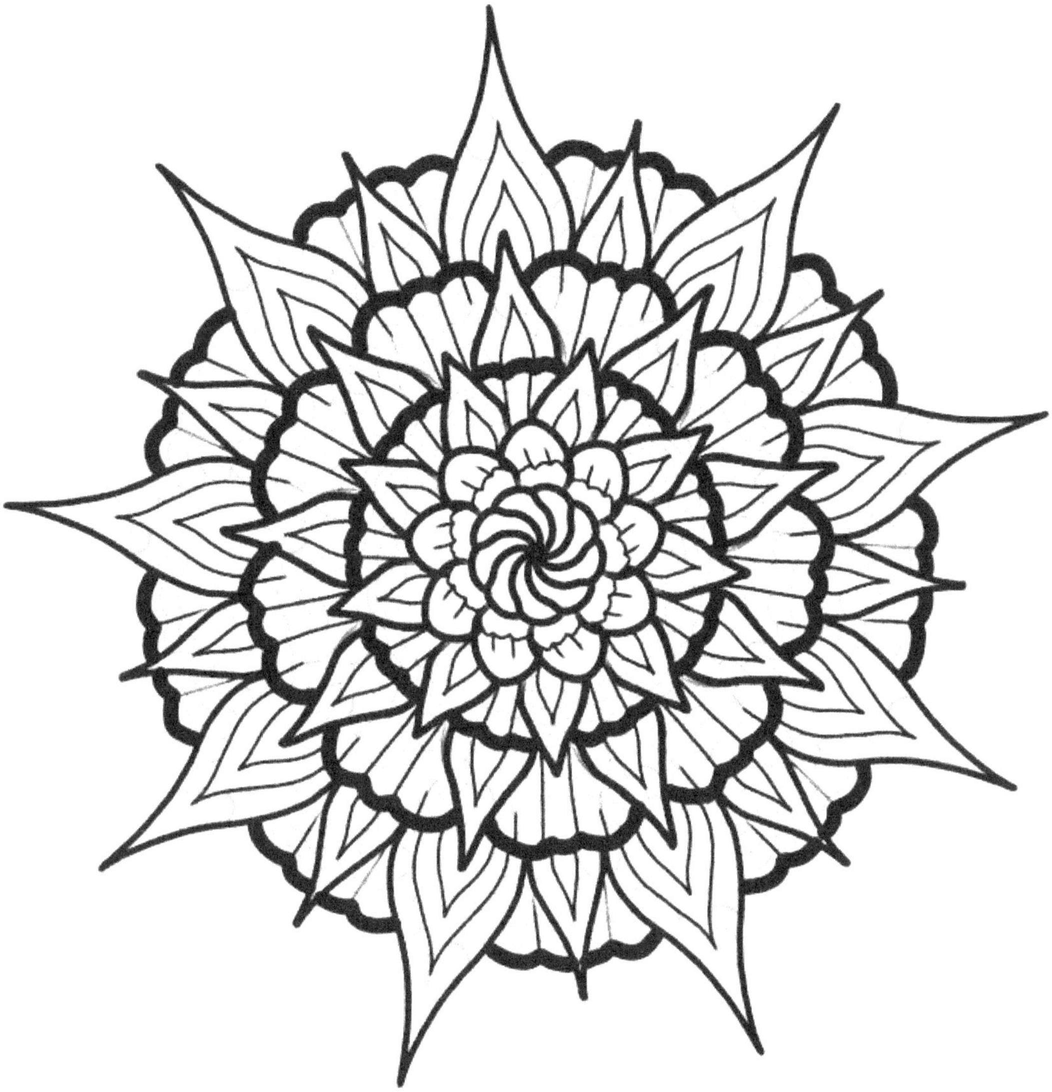

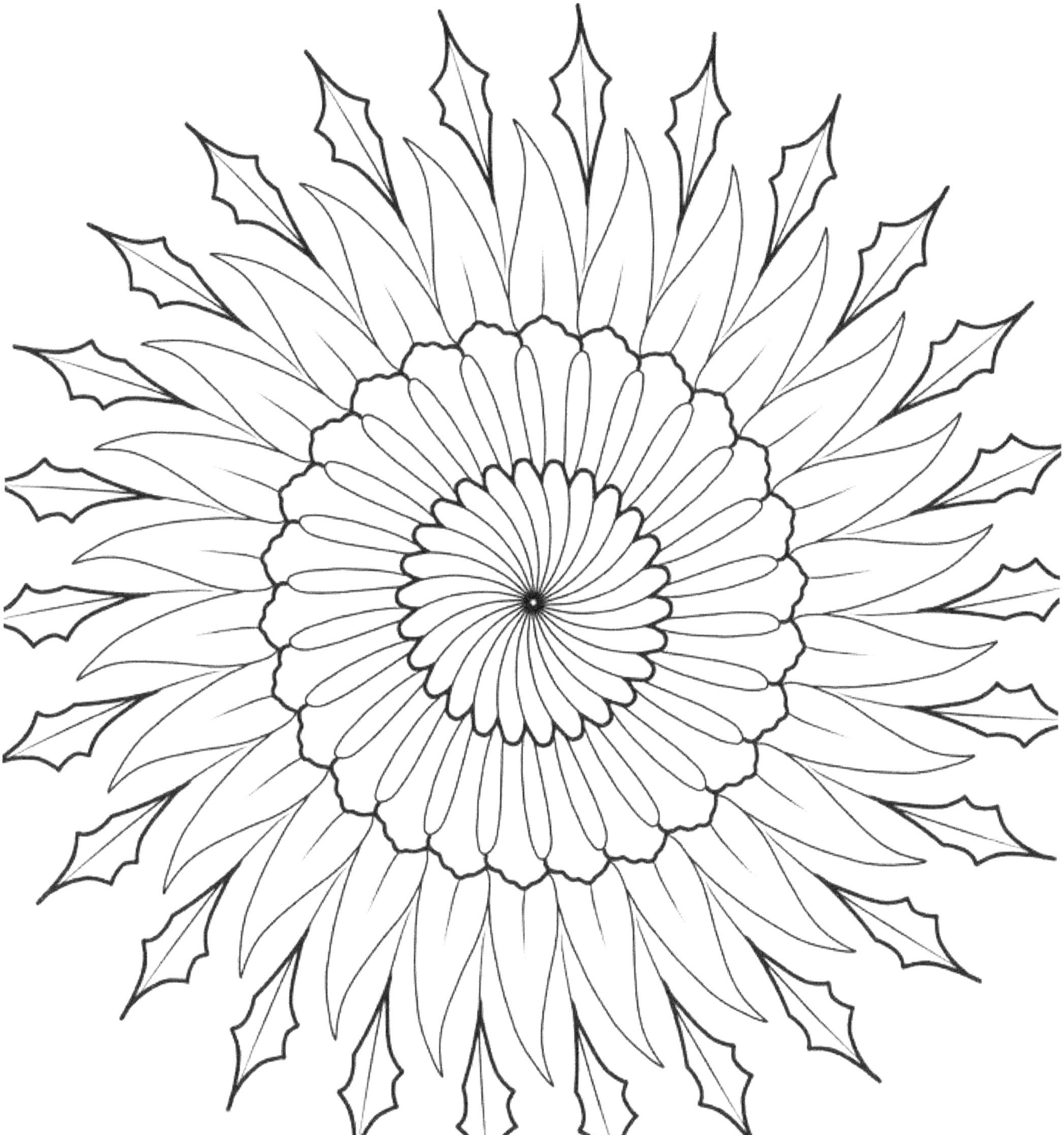

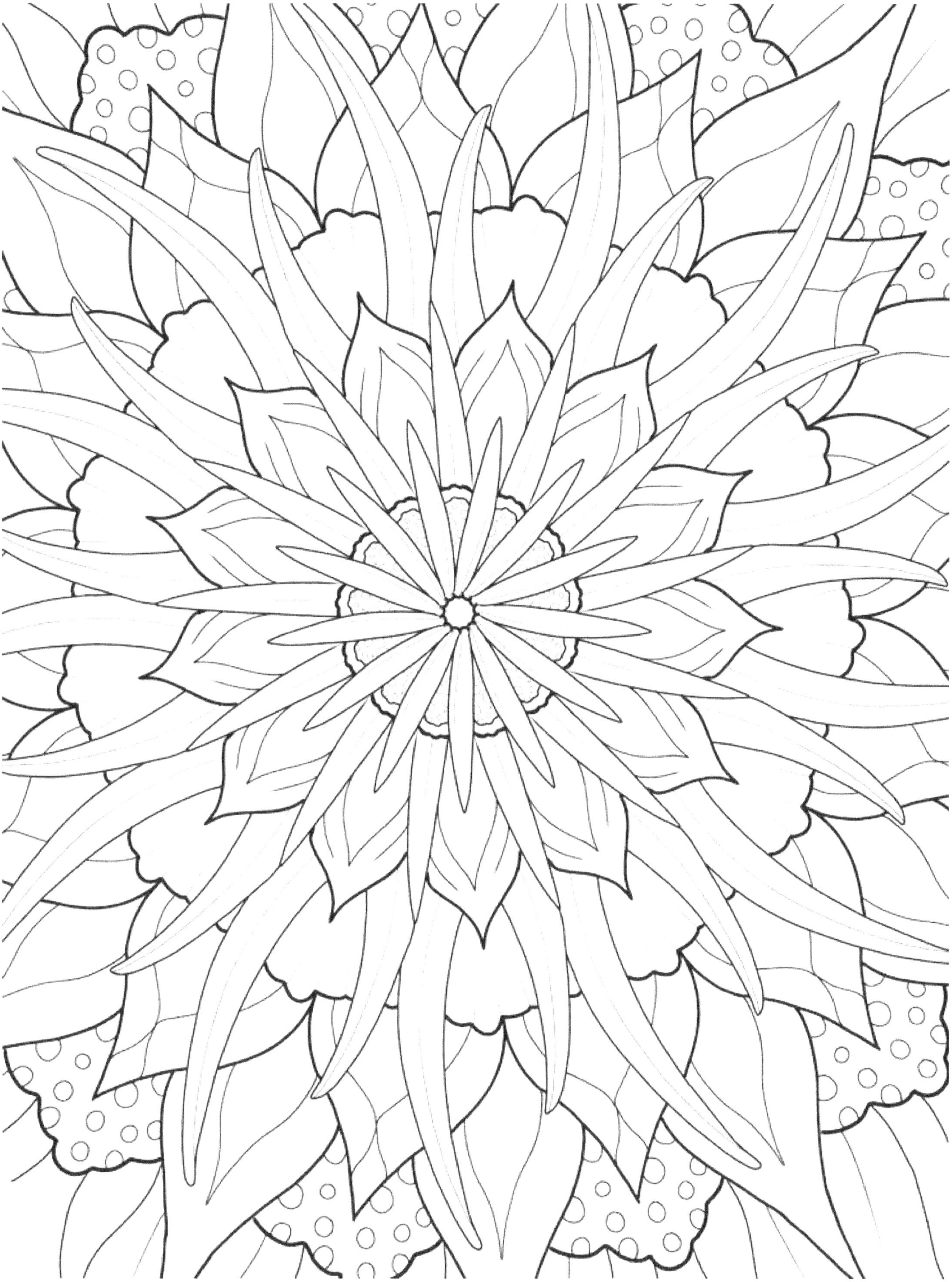

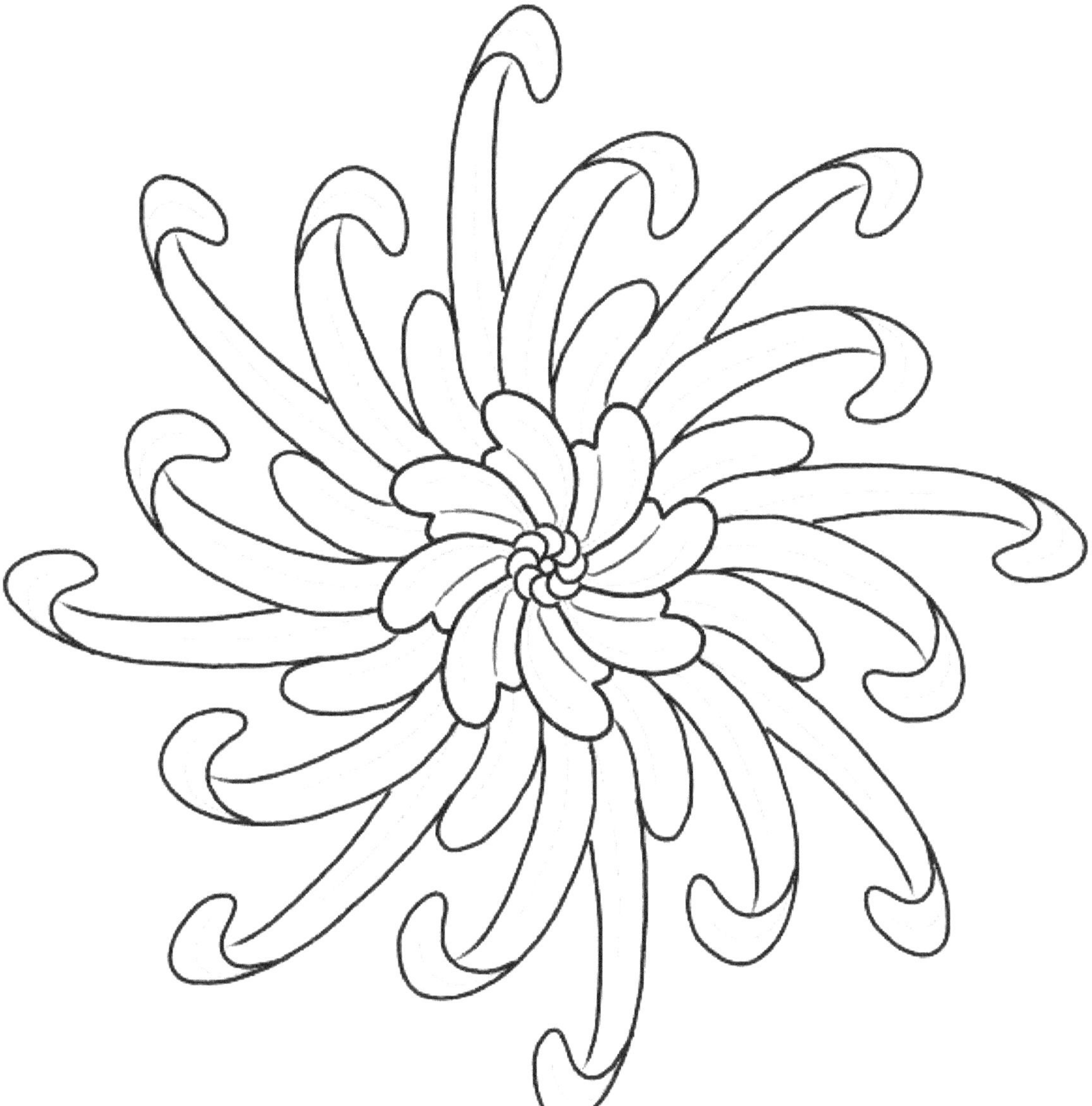

www.ingramcontent.com/pod-product-compliance
Lightning Source LLC
Chambersburg PA
CBHW080542190526
45169CB00007B/2600